18/15
23/17

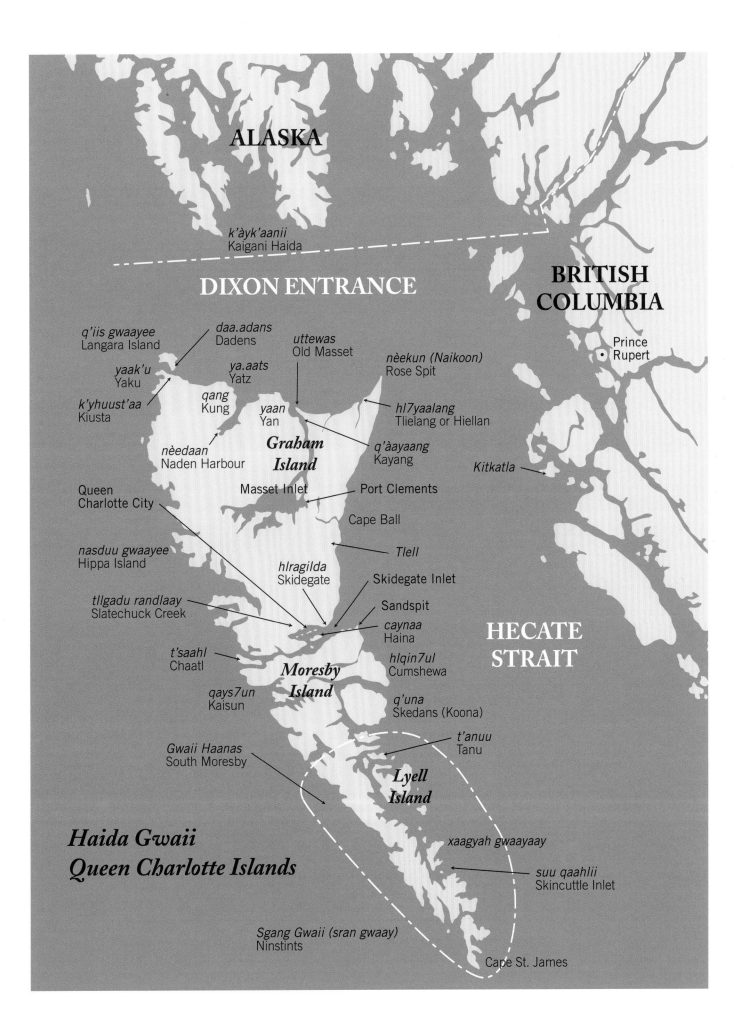

ALASKA

k'àyk'aanii
Kaigani Haida

DIXON ENTRANCE

BRITISH
COLUMBIA

• Prince
Rupert

q'iis gwaayee
Langara Island

daa.adans
Dadens

uttewas
Old Masset

nèekun (Naikoon)
Rose Spit

yaak'u
Yaku

ya.aats
Yatz

k'yhuust'aa
Kiusta

qang
Kung

yaan
Yan

hl7yaalang
Tlielang or Hiellan

nèedaan
Naden Harbour

*Graham
Island*

q'àayaang
Kayang

Kitkatla

Masset Inlet

Port Clements

Queen
Charlotte City

Cape Ball

nasduu gwaayee
Hippa Island

Tlell

hlragilda
Skidegate

Skidegate Inlet

tllgadu randlaay
Slatechuck Creek

Sandspit

t'saahl
Chaatl

caynaa
Haina

HECATE
STRAIT

*Moresby
Island*

hlqin7ul
Cumshewa

qays7un
Kaisun

q'una
Skedans (Koona)

Gwaii Haanas
South Moresby

t'anuu
Tanu

*Lyell
Island*

*Haida Gwaii
Queen Charlotte Islands*

xaagyah gwaayaay

suu qaahlii
Skincuttle Inlet

Sgang Gwaii (sran gwaay)
Ninstints

Cape St. James

Breathing Stone

Contemporary Haida Argillite Sculpture

CAROL SHEEHAN

Photography by Jack Litrell and John W. Heintz

Frontenac House
Calgary, Alberta

Published by

Frontenac House Ltd.
1138 Frontenac Avenue S.W.
Calgary, Alberta, T2T 1B6, Canada
www.FrontenacHouse.com

Library and Archives Canada Cataloguing in Publication

Sheehan, Carol
    Breathing stone : contemporary Haida argillite sculpture / Carol
Sheehan ; photography by Jack Litrell and John W. Heintz.

Includes bibliographical references and index.
ISBN 978-1-897181-21-8 (bound).--ISBN 978-1-897181-22-5 (pbk.)

    1. Haida sculpture. 2. Argillite--British Columbia--Queen Charlotte
Islands.
3. Haida artists--Biography. I. Litrell, Jack II. Heintz, John W. III. Title.

NB249.5.H34S44 2008   730.89'9728
C2008-902807-4

Book and cover design: Epix Design Inc.
Photography: Jack Litrell and John W. Heintz
Photographic art direction: Carol Sheehan

All customary diligent efforts have been made to obtain permission from
appropriate copyright holders to reproduce works and photographs published
in this book. In the event that any such work or photograph has not been
acknowledged, the publisher and author would appreciate information to
correct this omission in future editions.

Photographs in this book taken by Jack Litrell and John W. Heintz are copyright
Frontenac House. Copyright for photographs provided by Gary Piaget, Jeff
Gamble, Walter Stolting, Sophia K. Browne and Robert Giauque remain with
those persons respectively. Written permission must be obtained from the
copyright holders to reproduce or use these photographs in any way.

Frontenac House gratefully acknowledges the support of the Canada Council
for the Arts for our publishing program. We also gratefully acknowledge the
support of The Alberta Foundation for the Arts. Masters Gallery Limited of
Calgary, Alberta has provided invaluable advice and assistance without which
this book would not have been possible.

Canada Council   Conseil des Arts
for the Arts   du Canada

Alberta Foundation for the Arts

ACKNOWLEDGEMENTS

Breathing Stone is a collaborative work. To all those who have contributed to it—*howaa*, thank you. I am especially indebted to the artists and their families for welcoming us into their homes and studios, making time for long interviews, and allowing us to disrupt their daily lives with our presence and bundles of equipment.

The idea for this book germinated at Masters Gallery in Calgary during their 2005 exhibition of contemporary argillite sculpture. Many of the sculptures for the show were by Haida artists I did not know; many were toddlers when I wrote my first book on Haida argillite. Seeing their work, I was speechless with excitement at how fine it was. As a consultant to that exhibition, I renewed an old friendship with Sarah Hillis Davidson of Sarah's Arts and Jewellery in Old Masset. Before the exhibition opened, Sarah and I decided to collaborate on this book. Very quickly, Rod Green of Masters Gallery offered vital insights, enthusiasm, support and encouragement essential for making *Breathing Stone* a reality. My deepest thanks.

In 2006 Sarah co-coordinated my initial visits to argillite artists in Haida Gwaii. That fall, we took the idea to Frontenac House and developed a plan to publish *Breathing Stone*. Our next steps were contracting two photographers, Jack Litrell in Masset and John W. Heintz in Calgary, and charting our path through a myriad daunting logistics. In October 2007, John and I returned to Haida Gwaii to interview and photograph in Masset and Skidegate. In January 2008 we visited more studios, galleries, and private collections in B.C. and Alberta.

Our thanks to the private collectors and commercial galleries who kindly allowed us to rearrange their spaces to photograph their precious artworks. In particular we are grateful to Grace and John Ballem, to Kim McCormick, Sandy West, Wayne and Kimberly Skinner, Gordon and Marilyn Weber, Dr. Craig Spowart, Lloyd Audy, and Denis Haughey for permitting us to disrupt their homes with cameras and lights. Thank you to Gary Piaget and photographer Jeff Gamble for providing additional photographs. Many thanks to Robert Giauque who photographed pieces in private U.S. collections.

Special thanks to Svetlana Fouks, Raymond Kazemzadeh, and Dorothy Washbern of Coastal Peoples Fine Arts Gallery; Peter Lattimer, Alex Dawkins, and Cissy Chan at Lattimer Gallery; Douglas Reynolds, Kaitlan Lay, and Lakshmi McCall at Douglas Reynolds Gallery; Brandy Banman at Art of Man Gallery; and Laura Dutheil at Crystal Cabin Gallery in Tlell, Haida Gwaii. Walter Stolting sent images from Spirits of the Northwest Coast Native Arts Gallery in Comox. Howaa.

For amazing hospitality, thank you to: Barry and Gina Wood; Alice Williamsen and Lionel Samuels; Francis Jeffrey Pelletier; and Vicki and Soren Pedersen. Thanks also to matriarch Molly Yorke (*Ta'Ow King Ung Duus*) for the comfort of Haida Gwaii Lodge in Old Masset.

Robin K. Wright's comprehensive *Northern Northwest Coast Master Carvers* has been an invaluable resource for checking historical details and Haida spellings. Howaa. Sarah Hillis Davidson has verified much of the information concerning language, clan affiliations, and cultural insights. She opened her home to us and was a continual source of enthusiasm and encouragement.

To Jim Hart, Chief Edenshaw, of Old Masset—a canoe full of thanks. From this side of the Rockies, I have watched your apprenticeship to Bill Reid, celebrated your high achievements as a master carver, and cheered your artistic and cultural leadership on and off Haida Gwaii. Receiving your enthusiastic support for this book inspired us all. Your poem is a blessing for all the people so passionate about argillite art. Howaa from a full heart.

For David Scollard's editorial help I shall be eternally grateful. His love of art, ideas and words always inspires me. Howaa to designer Neil Petrunia who has a love of First Nations art. His design for this book is nothing short of extraordinary in its refreshing innovation. His insight and sensitivity, evident in every page, honour each artist.

Thank you to Jack Litrell for providing outstanding photographs in the natural settings of Haida Gwaii that are so close to his heart. In continually striving for excellence, Jack helped make *Breathing Stone* a unique visual experience.

I am deeply grateful to the publisher and fine staff of Frontenac House. Their vision, excitement and generosity have enriched every writer who has come under their protective and nurturing wings. Howaa for making this journey.

Thank you to my son, David, and my husband, John W. Heintz. You both were there for me every step of the way. John, your task quickly shifted from portraiture to creating many of the fine photographs in *Breathing Stone*. You rose to the challenge with energy, care and imagination. Thank you.

Howaa Salaana.

CONTENTS

The Trek of Old

Trucking, the weather?
Boat to take
Hiking, Birds, Forest, Mountains
River to cross & cross again,   Bears…the chance
Arrival, the joy of Arrival, The Pit
Plans, Looking, Searching, Decisions
Slabs to cut, cut of our special wonderful
      Black beautiful sparkling soft stone.
Working, sawing, sweating, the grime
the Load, the strain, the trek back
      The Laborious Trek
Arrival, Finally the shore.   Eagles.
The Boat
Trucking Home
Home
Celebration, Plans, Dreams, Stories to Tell
Dreams to Finish
Carve, Carve, Carve, Carve. Finally the
Finish.
People to meet, Sale to complete, Celebration
of the Exchange, things to do….
Dream & Dream again
Stories to tell, Shapes to Carve, Slate to
get, Plan the Trek, History to make.

James Hart
Chief Edenshaw
May 18/08

FOREWORD

Breathing Stone is devoted to 15 very individual contemporary Haida argillite sculptors. Based on interviews conducted in their studios, homes, and galleries, each chapter presents an intimate encounter with a single artist and his approach to this art form. Each story is a glimpse into the artist's life as he shares thoughts about his personal and cultural identity, his aesthetic sense and his place in the art world.

It is essential to understand that argillite is not for the faint of heart. Quarrying and transporting the stone off Slatechuck Mountain takes monumental effort and tremendous physical strength. There's no doodling in this stone; every argillite sculptor is committed to the medium and to the message well before carving begins—and that sometimes requires weeks of hard thinking. Creating a sculpture may take months as the artist draws upon complex themes and designs artistically challenging images. Carving argillite is risky and slow because the stone often harbours unpredictable and sometimes fatal flaws that can flake off or crack a sculpture in progress. Unlike carving in wood, there's nothing clean or fragrant about working argillite; the process ubiquitously coats studios, clothing, hands and lungs with a coal-like dust.

When the artwork is finished, bringing it to the marketplace is always a significant undertaking that requires planning, safe transport and careful coordination of buyer and seller. Because it takes such a long time to create an argillite sculpture, the artists generally seek immediate sales; few sculptors can afford to leave their work on consignment. Once a piece of sculpture reaches a point of sale, it commands a very high price in a specialized art niche.

Studying the art has its problems too. From the very beginning of this art form almost two centuries ago, the body of the work has been scattered worldwide into museums, galleries, and private collections. The logistics for gathering information and photographs are extremely daunting. Museums often feel constrained in exhibiting and travelling this sculpture because of the complex handling problems. Though some of the pieces reach public collections, much of the art remains sequestered in private hands, far from scholars' reach, removed from the public eye.

Yet despite argillite's inherent challenges and difficulties, everyone involved in the creation, possession, study and appreciation of argillite sculpture shares something in common—a deeply held passion for this incomparable Haida art. Focusing on contemporary Haida artists, *Breathing Stone* explores some of this passion.

Chapter One provides a brief history and analysis of argillite sculpture from contact times to the present. This is a story of Haida artists surviving and growing through periods of almost unthinkable cultural devastation until, with the development of a confident new generation of contemporary artists, a flourishing new stage of the art form has appeared.

Chapter Two explains some of the technical, conceptual and aesthetic considerations in shaping the stone and challenges the viewer not only to see argillite sculpture, but also to think about the fascinating, complex culture that resonates within it.

Chapter Three peers over the shoulder of Cooper Wilson as he transforms, step by step, a massive chunk of argillite into a finished sculpture. Watching this piece progress demonstrates first hand how Haida argillite artists conceive, manipulate and finish the stone, how they breathe life into their images.

The next chapters introduce 15 remarkable artists who sculpt in argillite. All are well known in their own communities, by collectors, and by the galleries who represent them throughout North America. There are many other artists working in argillite with commensurate talents and vision; we hope that *Breathing Stone* will not only encourage them and bring about creative dialogue, but that galleries and collectors will seek them out as well.

Learning about argillite and the sculptors who work in this medium is an opportunity to learn more about Haida Gwaii, its people, its culture and its language. Because Haida was not traditionally a written language, there are many ways to spell almost every word and little consensus on how that should be done. Masset, Skidegate and Alaskan Haida dialects, though mutually intelligible, are distinct enough to make the task of writing Haida even more difficult. The pre-eminent linguist John Enrico has written a massive two-volume dictionary of the Haida language, though this too is not yet in universal use. (Enrico, 2005)

Encountering written Haida will bring forth several questions, perhaps the most obvious of which is: why are so many Haida words written with the number **7** in them? In the early days of studying aboriginal languages, linguists strove to create orthographies that could be recorded using an ordinary typewriter keyboard; as a result, the glottal stop, which was formally transcribed as a symbol resembling a question mark without the dot, was typed as the numeral **7**. Thus some written Haida words contained a **7** to indicate a glottal stop in the spoken word, a style that has been retained by many current writers.

Haida words appear in the text and index as they have been provided by the artists and local language specialists, as well as by contemporary scholars. When current spellings were not available, we used words as transcribed by John Swanton, the first linguist to write down Haida as it was spoken at the turn of the last century. Haida words have been reproduced as they were provided to us in the hope that, despite the variety and inconsistencies in spelling, the transcriptions would approximate spoken Haida and help non-Haida persons appreciate the richness of this language without having to consult and cross-reference lengthy and complicated orthographies.

Intellectually we know there is more to life than art and language, but when we think about artists we rarely think beyond their artwork and about their daily lives and relationships, especially if we haven't lived in their culture. *Breathing Stone* is not intended to be an exhaustive or encyclopaedic work – rather it is an introduction to and an appreciation of a unique and vital contemporary art as shown through the works, words and lives of 15 artists. All of the argillite artists included in this book are men of vision, skill and competence, residing locally on the Northwest Coast, but living globally.

In *Breathing Stone* we hope you will find, perhaps for the first time—and then continue to nourish—a passion for argillite and the artists who sculpt it. Through their images and stories, may you grow in appreciating the vibrant message of all that it means to be Haida.

14

This book is dedicated to the children of Haida Gwaii.
Howaa Salaana

For almost two centuries, Haida carvers in argillite have created an impressive body of work that constitutes one of the strongest continuous traditions in the history of Canadian art. Produced by survivors of both disease and acculturation, argillite images are fundamental to understanding a uniquely Haida history of ideas. These images in the soft black stone—a black carbonaceous shale the Haida term *kwawhlahl* (also written *qwa.a s7a laa*), meaning "soft stone"—are testimonies to a cherished and vibrantly alive culture.

A century ago, in 1905, Haida consultants explained to John R. Swanton, an ethnologist from the American Museum of Natural History, that their islands home, Haida Gwaii, was the centre of an ancient and richly populated world. Linguistically and culturally, the *Xay'de* or *Xaadaa 7laa Iss* ("The Good People") were divided into four major branches. The southern people lived in now-abandoned villages on the islands they called *Gwaii Haanas*, the central groups were located primarily in Skidegate, the northern group resides in Old Masset, and the Alaskan or *Kaigani* people make their homes primarily in the Prince of Wales Archipelago.

In the early years of Euro-American seafaring exploration, British sailors renamed the islands after their monarch Queen Charlotte, ignorant of the fact that these sacred places were filled with a host of natural and supernatural spirits animating the forces and events of the cosmos. Swanton had much to learn and his Haida teachers passed on a wealth of knowledge.

In the beginning, the Haida patiently explained to Swanton, Haida Gwaii (literally, Land of the People) floated at the centre of an orb; above hung the sky—a solid firmament shaped like an inverted bowl to which the celestial bodies were loosely fastened. (Swanton, 1905a:12).

The upper world or sky-country was layered into a prestigious "five-row town". There lived the mightiest supernatural being, Power-of-the-Shining-Heavens *(Sins sqa'nagwa-i)*, who gave powers to most of the other supernatural beings in the Haida cosmos. (Swanton, 1905a:12). Beneath the land, an important spirit, Sacred-One-Standing-and-Moving *(Qo'yagiagA'ndal)* provided the firm foundation for Haida Gwaii and supported the sky above by balancing a pole on his chest. The Haida prayer sung to this spirit shows a conscious and respectful relationship between the people, their islands, and Haida Gwaii's supernatural inhabitants: "Upon your good land let me live long." (Swanton, 1905a:12–13; 23).

The seas too were filled with spirits. Ocean People *(Tsagan xaayda-gaay)* lived in human-type habitations in villages below the sea. Some of the marine spirits gave their bodies to humans for food and then regenerated new bodies from pieces of the old that had been transported to their supernatural homes through fire or water. The most powerful of

SONGS OF SEA AND SKY
Songs of Haida Gwaii

the Ocean People were the Killer Whale People, known as *sqa'na* or *sraa.n* (Dawson, 1880:122B). Human life was made possible through the generosity of the supernatural life cycle.

The natural and the supernatural often merged. For example, supernatural beings could have a dual character: a human form that could be altered at will into an animal shape by the mere donning of a coat of fur, feathers, fins or some other appropriate disguise. Supernatural beings could entertain, marry, and otherwise assist humans. Not always benevolent, on occasion they might hinder, tease, or even harm humankind. As animals—birds, salmon, herring, black whales, bears—they were called *Gi'na te'iga;* as supernatural entities—Eagle People, Salmon People, Herring People, Black Whale People, Bear People— they were collectively *Sga'na qeda's,* literally, "Those for Whom Land was First Created" (Swanton, 1905a: 13, 16–17).

At the beginning of time, the personification of Raven, the most conspicuous character in Haida stories, was called Slender One or He whose Voice is Obeyed (*NAñkî'lsLas* or *Nang kilsdlaas*). Some of Swanton's Haida teachers maintained that Raven was a great man, a founder of the human species (as one story goes, he discovered the Haida people in a clamshell) and its principal benefactor. Raven brought light, fire, water and other life-sustaining commodities to the people. Only as a voracious trickster did Nang kilsdlaas don his bird identity. He then went under different names: *Yaahl, Yehl* or *Xuyaa.* Still other Haida explained that Raven was a great figure in the beginning of time, but later became corrupt.

Eagle, Raven's companion in the Skidegate stories, was a second supernatural hero who also figured prominently in the early days of creation before humans came into existence. (Swanton, 1905a: 28; 1905b:28). In the Masset stories, Butterfly was Raven's companion. Both Eagle and Butterfly have supporting roles in Raven's primordial antics, and like Raven, are not responsible for creating beneficial features of the world so much as causing them to happen.

The Haida have always based their social and political organizations on the principle of matrilineal descent, which means that wealth, social rank and some aspects of spiritual position are inherited through the female side of families.

Haida lineages to this day are aligned into two clans: the Ravens and the Eagles. According to Swanton's teachers, the Eagles trace their origins to the supernatural ancestress or "powerful grandmother", *Djila'qons* or Copper Woman, wife of Nang kilsdlaas. The opposite clan, the Ravens, regard Foam Woman or "She of the Powerful Face" as their founder. Marriage could occur only between people of opposite clans. This rule, strictly enforced, meant that in traditional Haida society, a person of Raven descent must marry a person from the Eagle clan.

The Haida clans celebrate their traditional heritage in the visual images, stories, and songs of their inherited and publicly validated crests, but not every lineage, family or individual is entitled to every crest image, name or song. Crests are inherited by individuals through the matrilineal line and trace a series of social as well as supernatural events. Some of the Raven crests are: Raven, Grizzly Bear, Rainbow, Cirrus Cloud, Cumulus Cloud, Sea Lion, Dogfish, Wolf, Flicker, Thunderbird or Blue Hawk, Killer Whale, Snag or Sea Grizzly *(Tc A'mos)*, Black Bear, Mountain Goat, Moon, and *Gitga'lgia* or "Child of Property Woman". Predominant Eagle crests are: Eagle, Raven (received from a Tsimshian family), Dogfish, Cormorant, Beaver, Frog, Sculpin, Halibut, Whale, Copper, Weasel, Sea Wolf *(Wasgo)*, Hummingbird, and Five-finned Killer Whale (Swanton, 1905a: 114–115; 108). These crests—and the stories of the natural and supernatural spirits associated with them—form the basis of the imagery in argillite sculpture from its inception in the early part of the 19th century to the present.

Owning and displaying a crest is an individual's way of making visible and public a personal history and links to a specific clan by relating how the crest was obtained and the privileges that accompany it. Crests, in traditional Haida society, were displayed in and on sophisticated architecture, on their monumental sculpture, on ceremonial objects—masks, rattles, dancing blankets, frontlet headdresses—as well as on objects of everyday life such as spoons, storage boxes, fish hooks, bowls and canoes. Often sacred and profane arts were combined, creating a visually and aurally rich landscape, evidence of high cultural achievement.

The Haida excelled in the visual arts. Products of Haida artists abound in museums around the globe—an astonishing fact given that these "objects of bright pride," as curator Allen Wardwell once described them, came from a culture whose population numbered only in the thousands. Anthropologist Wilson Duff described the Haida as "the most maritime and the most intensely artistic" of all the Northwest Coast First Nations (Duff, 1967:n.p.). Island people, they journeyed great distances to trade and to visit, as well as to make war. Haida canoes and carved chests were much sought after by other First Nations peoples, and Haida artists travelled widely to fulfill artistic commissions.

From the earliest Euro-American visitors to Haida Gwaii—Juan Pérez's Spanish voyage in 1774—to the present day, outsiders have collected cultural accounts and examples of Haida artistic endeavours and have placed them in collections and archives around the world. Initially, contact with outside cultures brought an economic and cultural flowering on the coast as new markets, products and ideas were introduced at a pace the First Nations could absorb. The Haida, displaying an awesome acumen for business, were at the vanguard of these early economic opportunities. The maritime fur trade was characterized by a brief economic prosperity that lasted from Pérez's visit until around 1804.

It was not long, however, before the fluorescence dimmed. The strangers were here to stay. Increasing numbers of Euro-American seamen, traders, missionaries and settlers pushed their way onto the North Pacific coasts, bringing new products and new technologies. This imposing presence, while stimulating some aspects of aboriginal life, dramatically changed or extinguished others. The Haida population, roughly estimated at 8,400 people up until the 1850s, dropped to 6,000 in less than a generation (Dawson, 1880:166; Duff, 1964:39).

Far more devastating than these cultural blows were the epidemics of smallpox and other infectious diseases that swept up the coast in 1862. Within the astonishingly short span of three years, most Northwest Coast indigenous populations were diminished by a third (Duff, 1964:39). The most seriously affected by the smallpox epidemic were the Haida, who declined from almost 6,000 people to about 1,000. By 1885, the British Columbia census recorded only 800 Haida; by 1915, in less than a generation, only 588 Haida remained (Duff and Kew, 1958; Duff, 1964: 38-39). Their near-annihilation is inadequately recorded in historical texts, but Haida memory of the devastation persists in the oral tradition to this day. It has taken nearly a century for their numbers to increase to a level that is still fewer than 4,000 Haida living in Haida Gwaii.

Many Haida arts declined almost as rapidly as the population. Villages containing massive cedar houses with their legendary "forests of totem poles" were abandoned. Disease silenced throats: the Haida language suffered, songs and stories became other peoples' collectors' items. The remaining population was too small to support the creation of the massive poles, large bent boxes, chiefs' seats, and other emblems of rank and wealth that characterized Haida art and culture. Elaborate ceremonials—especially the potlatches (*7waahlal*) that were necessary to validate every social and sacred prerogative and position—succumbed to the lack of population and eventually to foreigners' laws and religion (Dawson, 1880:171B; 175B; Niblack, 1888:242B). In 1884 the Canadian Government passed legislation to prohibit potlatching; the law was not repealed until 1951.

Traditional arts, especially the visual arts of carving, weaving and painting that had adorned every feature of cultural life, almost ceased as the Haida slipped toward the vortex of acculturation. The government policy of assimilation removed ceremonial regalia from the remaining villages and deported children to residential schools in an effort to erase the language, religion and culture. Often what remained became ethnographic artifacts in foreign treasure houses.

One of the greatest exceptions to this downward spiral was the ongoing production of argillite sculpture. Haida artists, as evidenced by the number of argillite pieces in world collections, remained prolific. Why did this happen?

A fundamental reason that Haida carvers continued their creative output was that the market remained constant. From the beginning, argillite sculpture was an art for export only. (The earliest museum documentation of an argillite artifact dates to 1818 in Berlin.) Argillite sculptures, images borne of rapidly changing times that responded to an encroaching Euro-American culture, were constantly being carried to the outside world. Created exclusively for sale to foreigners, these sculptures were sold for cash or traded for goods almost as quickly as they were made.

At first, the early argillite sculptors, living in a time of plenty and confident in their own culture, used whatever imagery suited their customers. While their images were similar to those on their great crest poles and house fronts, the Haida artists scrambled traditional figures and crests, unwilling to share the true foundational images of their cultural identity. While the marketplace was defined outside Haida Gwaii, the subject matter and the meanings of the sculptures were apparently not part of the purchase price, indeed were probably not even taken into consideration. The scant museum documentation for argillite collections suggests that buyers were more interested in the art's origins than in its iconography.

Later, the Haida artists portrayed Euro-American material culture and people in argillite art, mimicking the newcomers' clay and meerschaum pipes with the bowls adorned by faces. The Haida elongated the argillite pipes into thin panels, incorporating images of the foreigners, their pets and bits of the strange new architecture that was growing on the coast. They made elaborate circle and leaf designs on plates, platters, teacups, and cutlery whimsically reproduced in argillite. The otherness of the other people was often portrayed with humour, if not bewilderment. The argillite sculptures were amusing souvenirs and the Euro-Americans bought them all. Cold stone images were exchanged for money—one of the key forces of change in a culture that had previously known only a barter and subsistence economy.

Then the tragedy struck. After the epidemics the Haida population was reduced to one-tenth of what it had been in the early days of contact. While almost every aspect of their culture changed, argillite carving remained as a souvenir art, encouraged by governments and churches as a viable cottage industry for a shifting consumer economy.

This was not, however, a frivolous or meaningless direction in the art. Haida artists ceased creating fanciful argillite images of Euro-American curiosities. Instead, they launched into a new era of preserving all that it meant to be Haida as they introduced authentic crests and stories into their art. Unable to celebrate their life and culture in monumental works, they preserved their history in argillite sculptures and sold them to the collectors, sending the message of being Haida to the world and to the future. Argillite art became postcards to the universe, visual time capsules launched to people and places far from Haida Gwaii.

Today, much has changed. Over the last half-century, the Haida people have revitalized their visual arts and ceremonial traditions as the population has slowly increased. Many Haida have supplemented traditional food gathering with work in boat building, the commercial fishery and other trades. They have taken advantage of educational opportunities, seeking education themselves as well as educating outsiders. The Haida have found work with agencies in archaeology and natural resource management. Tourism to the ancient sites and monuments prompted a self-conscious political movement within the Haida Nation to preserve and protect the cultural heritage of *Gwaii Haanas* (South Moresby), its ecology and the old growth forests. That movement has expanded to protect all of Haida Gwaii and its surrounding seas.

The Haida are making valiant attempts to restore their ancient language. Through the work of linguists and programs generated by the Haida themselves, the spoken language is being recorded and taught. Though the population of native speakers dwindles with every passing of an elder, Haida songs are being sung and composed again; old Haida dances and new ones are being performed.

The art has expanded with the population. Along with other peoples of the Northwest Coast, Haida artists have taken advantage of and promoted an interest in "native art" that includes rendering traditional designs in a variety of media from painting and sculpture to limited-edition silkscreen prints, and creating original jewellery. For decades now, people have spoken of a renaissance of art on the Northwest Coast, and nowhere is it more evident than in Haida Gwaii.

As modern Haida artists began expanding their repertoire for the outside market, engraving gold and silver and carving larger pieces in cedar, some of the older traditions were revived. In turn, the market responded with a new respect for the traditional arts of weaving in spruce root, cedar bark, and mountain goat wool. And finally there was enough wealth for the first crest poles to be raised in Skidegate and Old Masset in over a century.

Haida artists are carrying the message of Haida culture around the world, fulfilling demands for monumental works in Japan, Chicago, Washington D.C., England, Germany and many other places. Museums that once had poles cut down from abandoned villages and transported continents away are now commissioning Haida artists to create new works to stand beside the old ones. These artists are returning to their villages with new wealth, a new sense of place and purpose as they create ceremonial regalia, raise crest poles, build canoes and longhouses, and host potlatch celebrations.

These are modern artists, well-versed in the traditions and techniques of western art history and its own modern movements. There is a new freedom for Haida artists to push the envelope of the "traditional" and explore ideas about realism, expressionism and abstractionism as they challenge the past and the future. These artists are willing to take artistic chances, to transcend time and place in their arts.

The visual artworks of many Haida artists are now on display in galleries and art museums, rather than only in museums of anthropology and natural history. Haida sculpture, paintings, drawings, engraving, silk-screen prints, and weaving are seen as unique and personal expressions of individuals, of named artists. The art continues to change in the hands of new and creative artists—in visual forms and in song.

Throughout the lean years and the years of revitalization, argillite sculpture has continued, waxing and waning in market popularity, but in 200 years, never ceasing. It has persisted as a uniquely Haida expression, moving from the status of souvenir curio to acceptance as high art. After years of intense study and interest, scholars and collectors have identified individual argillite masters of the past and related stylistic changes in the art to periods in Haida history. While we may never know the names of those distinguished past masters of carving argillite, we are privileged to know them through their stylistic signatures and to witness their brilliance and skill. Today, contemporary argillite sculptors are recognized and honoured by name, by their body of work, and by their reputation for excellence in the fine arts.

Argillite art bears witness to a poignant and evolving cultural history that saw the Haida push their way of life through a disastrous brush with near extinction into the 21st century. Argillite carving, uniquely Haida, is still primarily an art destined for ownership by non-Haida people. It still speaks eloquently, through many voices, to audiences worldwide, echoing songs from Haida Gwaii, songs of sea and sky, songs from the Land of the People.

SHAPING STONE:
Seeing and Thinking about Argillite Sculpture

Argillite sculpture is good to see and good to think. In fact, most contemporary Haida artists will tell you true enjoyment of this unique art requires more than a cursory reading of form and meaning; contemplation—focussing our thoughts to interact with the artist's thoughts—brings intimacy to what we see. In the thinking comes deeper comprehension of an artist and a culture, an appreciation that leaves us richer for the encounter.

Thinking about sculpture first brings to mind such practical questions as what materials are employed, how they are gathered and the tools used in creating it. These are important questions to ask about sculpture in general. More specifically, though, to understand northern Northwest Coast art, an appreciation of the fundamental elements of two- and three-dimensional design—called formline design—is essential. With that awareness, the questions about images and meaning, style and context, time and place become much more useful in providing insight into the artistic process, and ultimately into the artist as a thinking person.

What is argillite?

Beyond the obvious observation that it's a stone that Haida artists carve, there are some interesting geological and cultural facts—and fictions—about argillite that will help us appreciate this sculptural form. Called *kwawhlahl* (also written *qwa.a s7a laa*) in the Skidegate dialect, it is pronounced with a very soft 'g' in English: "ar-gil-lite". The word is derived from the adjective *argillaceous* (from *argil*, meaning "clay") and describes the fine-grained sedimentary rock that is transitional between slate and shale. Interestingly, the Haida word means "soft rock" and the colloquial term for argillite has long been "slate".

Since the beginning of the 19th century, argillite has been quarried on the northeastern slope of Slatechuck Mountain in the basin of Slatechuck Creek *(Tlgaduu randlaay)* on Graham Island between Chaatl *(Ts'aa7ahl 'llnagaay)* and Skidegate *(Hlragilda 'llnagaay)*. Since 1941, the Haida have maintained a strict tradition of legal ownership of the quarry, and the argillite of Haida Gwaii is reserved for the sole use of Haida artists.

Note that the Haida don't use the word "black" to name this carbonaceous stone. That too reflects a colloquial wisdom, for while the argillite the Haida quarry and carve is black to dark grey due to its slight carbon content, there are other hues of argillite found in different parts of the Northwest Coast and indeed throughout the world. Red Haida argillite sculptures are found in several museum collections and there is a single green example in Denver. The Haida sources of coloured argillite, if they are known, are not only rare, but are a well-kept secret. Red argillite is essentially *catlinite*, a type of soft stone coloured by oxidized hematite that is found primarily in Pipestone, Minnesota. Like Haida argillite, catlinite is soft enough to be hand carved and may be polished to a high gloss. Plains artists also have a long tradition of carving elaborate pipes and other sculptures in this stone.

It is an often-repeated fiction that argillite is only found in Haida Gwaii. Given their well-established cultural reputation for being astute entrepreneurs, it's neither unkind nor unrealistic to suggest that Haida carvers have deliberately enhanced the value of their medium with such stories to attract collectors. Rather, it is a fascinating marketing coup that for nearly 200 years they have protected their exclusive proprietary interests in carving argillite to the extent that no other Northwest Coast artists carve or attempt to market any stone art. In the art world, the word "argillite" is practically synonymous with Haida.

How is argillite made into sculpture?

After argillite is pried from the damp mossy hillside, it is soft enough to be cut with a handsaw. The work isn't easy, for although argillite is a relatively "soft" stone when compared to granite or marble, it is much harder than soapstone, which is mostly talc rich in magnesium. Talc has the lowest rating of 1 on the Mohs hardness scale; argillite ranks at 2.5; a diamond rates highest at 10 (Macnair and Hoover, 1984:15). Once the rock is sawn into large pieces, it has to be backpacked down the mountain—an arduous and slippery descent even without 75–100 pounds of rock weighing down the trekker. Older artists—and, some might contend, wiser—choose to pay younger Haida to obtain the raw argillite for them.

From as far back as 1874, writers have repeatedly asserted that argillite must be kept moist while being carved and that the finished sculpture becomes hard and un-carvable as it dries. Art historian and curator Bill Holm succinctly clarified this idea:

There is a widespread story that the material when first quarried is very soft (some versions imply that it can almost be modeled like clay) and that it hardens on exposure to the air until it resists all efforts to carve it. These stories are probably based on the fact that argillite…is wet when quarried and tends to split into slabs if it is allowed to dry too rapidly. For this reason, the carvers protect their stock…by burying it or sealing the end grain with shellac. It may become slightly more brittle upon drying, but the difference in hardness between fresh argillite and long dried—even century-long dried—argillite is practically undetectable (Holm 1972:86).

Once it reaches the artists, argillite is shaped and carved with a wide variety of tools: gravers, gouges, chisels, and knives. Some of these are hand-made, fashioned from iron files and stainless steel knives; some are purchased commercially; and some are adapted to argillite carving from other applications, such as dental tools. It is not uncommon for the bases of very large pieces to be quickly levelled with a belt sander. It takes great skill to engrave a curved line in argillite with a chisel or knife. Often the blade must make several passes along the same line to produce a flawless smooth cut without chipped edges. Argillite is not whittled like wood, but rather is painstakingly shaved and gently shaped with finer and finer cutting tools. There are few chips of argillite surrounding an artist—more likely the artist and his surroundings will be coated with a ubiquitous film of fine dust.

Argillite can flake and break—usually at the most inopportune times in the carving process—as the stone may be riddled with hidden fissures and tiny ribbons of other mineral deposits. When that happens, the old-timers used to reach for a glue made from boiling fish skins that, once applied, took days to dry. Today, virtually every Haida carver's remedy for cracks and flakes is a tube of cyanoacrylate (the generic name for Superglue® or Krazy Glue®), a fast-drying, tenacious adhesive particularly suited to materials such as argillite that contain minute traces of moisture. Only a skilled conservator or preferably the artist should ever attempt to repair an argillite sculpture.

Argillite artists use a variety of inlay materials in their sculpture. Some are obtained locally in Haida Gwaii, while lapidary shops and traders on the mainland supply other materials. The most common are: Californian or New Zealand abalone shell with its iridescent colours of deep blue, green and purple; iridescent mother-of-pearl from mollusc shells; Alaskan mastodon (fossil) ivory varying in colour from off-white to golden brown; large marine mammal teeth purchased in shops or harvested from carcasses washed up on shore; fossilized walrus tusk; and catlinite in hues ranging from delicate pinks to deep rose. Some artists use camel bone, copper, silver and gold for inlay and, less frequently, whole teeth from a chum salmon *(Oncorhynchus keta)*. Argillite sculpture also has been combined with engraved silver, gold and wood components or bases. Inlays are usually planned and executed before the piece is entirely completed.

Each artist has a personal preference when it comes to the appearance of his argillite sculptures. Tool finishing—the application of fine parallel lines shaving each surface to produce a smooth finish—seems to have been the preference in the early years of argillite production. After 1890, the fashion was to use fine abrasives to polish out any tool marks on the stone, followed by the application of oil-based graphite mixtures or black shoe polish to add a deep black luster to the surfaces (Macnair and Hoover, 1984:15). Contemporary artists may still polish their work with the finest emery cloth, but many have reverted to the labour-intensive but highly pleasing tool finish.

What is formline design?

The distinctive elements of northern Northwest Coast design that artists had used for centuries were first given formal names and definitions by Bill Holm in his 1965 book *Northwest Coast Indian Art: An Analysis of Form*. In it he described not only the elements of two-dimensional design but also the relationships between them that constitute the "rules" or, more properly, the conventions in the art.

The foundation of his description was the *formline*: that almost calligraphic line used by Northwest Coast artists that begins from a point as a thin line, swells into a thicker line with a single pulse, and then diminishes again. The elements of formline design are all based on the idea of the formline as a "sweeping line-like figure" that structures all forms. Every formline is separated from other formlines by a controlled space that defines and balances the relationship between those formlines.

The convention is that when one formline element meets another, one shrinks or gives way to the dominant line. When two thick formlines come together, the artist relieves what could be a heavy, thick convergence by introducing at that junction a space in the shape of a circle, a crescent, a Y or a T. Formline designs are constructed with primary and secondary formlines, each having a "weight" or thickness that defines it as the major or supporting element of the overall design. The primary and secondary formlines are usually painted black and red respectively; in Haida designs on wood and in silkscreen prints, tertiary elements such as eye sockets are often painted blue-green.

The dominant shape in Northwest Coast design Holm called the *ovoid*. This circular or oval form is made by connecting the two ends of a formline so that the form begins with a small line, swells to a thick line, then curves around to return to its starting point with an equally small line.

23

1: Three-dimensional ovoid on Raven's wing on *Journey of the Spirit Canoe* by Sean Brennan.

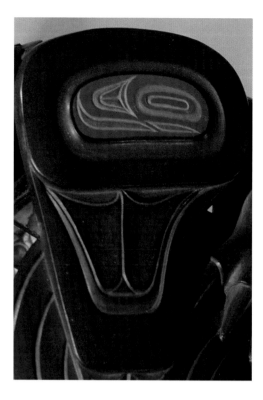

Ovoids come in all shapes, from nearly perfectly round to sausage-like forms. Ovoids are used to delineate the eyes, joints of the body (ankles, knees, shoulders, hips, etc.), palms of hands, whale blowholes, tail joints. They give shape to the heads of some animals and humans. Thus, wherever an ovoid appears, there is an opportunity to create a visual pun by having it form a joint or a face or both. There are several examples of different ovoids on the Eagle design on Gary Minaker Russ's *Supernatural Man Who Married the Eagle King's Daughter*, for instance.

Ovoids are almost always "filled" with another non-concentric element: a solid ovoid or a design element called a *salmon-trout head*, which consists of either the profile of a face having an eyebrow, eye, curled snout, lip and/or teeth; or a full frontal view of a face. The wing ovoid from Darrell White's *Raven and Clam Shell Pipe* is filled with an inner ovoid space and salmon-trout head in catlinite. Below it is a large primary U-form filled or "stacked" with an inner split U-form.

In formline design, the ovoids are connected to other design elements by two other forms. U-forms and S-forms resemble the letters that name them. They may be rendered as outlined borders or in solid shapes. The U-form is a formline with parallel diminishing lines. The S-form has the diminishing lines stretching away from each other in opposite directions. U-forms, for example, may be inverted and used to define ears, or stacked and used to define feathers. Similarly, S-forms can be used to

2: (Above) Catlinite salmon-trout head in wing ovoid on *Raven and Clam Shell* panel pipe by Darrell White.

3: (Below) Elongated and round ovoids on *Supernatural Man Who Married the Eagle King's Daughter* by Gary Minaker Russ.

detail limbs or stacked to depict a ribcage. The U-forms and S-forms may be further elaborated by introducing a split into their shapes. In *Shark Woman Dancing*, Donnie Edenshaw uses S-forms and split S-forms on the blanket's shark design to indicate the ribcage.

The design field brings in anatomical elements—eyelid lines, eyebrows, eye sockets, tongues, claws, hands, feet, noses, ears, feathers and fins—that may be rendered in formlines or may be solid shapes or lines. Anatomical elements such as hands and feet may be connected by U-forms and S-forms to the main figure, a technique that can imply gesture or movement.

Initially, Holm described two-dimensional formline design as being extended into three dimensions by wrapping the design around a preexisting form. Ultimately, however, he recognized that two-dimensional and three-dimensional "are so interrelated that it is at times hard to say where one ends and another begins." (Holm, 1965:14). That is precisely what happens in argillite sculpture: formlines are carved as fully three-dimensional forms distinguished by width and depth, and though they are not painted (as in two-dimensional designs), they have a definite relationship with one another. In argillite sculpture there is no "negative" or empty space, just dimensional formlines that are united and balanced through their relationships to one another. All the formlines in Gary Minaker Russ's *Su'san* sculpture have been created as fully three-dimensional forms.

4: (Above) Gary Minaker Russ, *Su'san* sculpture.

5: (Below) S-forms alternate with split S-forms in the shark's body on Donnie Edenshaw's *Shark Woman Dancing* sculpture.

25

Bill Holm's analysis of form augmented our earlier understanding of the conventions Northwest Coast artists used to portray certain animals, humans and supernatural beings. For example, most animals including birds are portrayed with ears over the forehead. Humans are shown with ears alongside the head or concealed beneath hair; frogs are rarely shown with ears. The length of the beak marks the difference between an eagle (sharply down-turned beak) and a raven (long slender beak). Animals in transformation may be shown with both animal and human attributes. Sea mammals and fish have distinctive tails, pectoral and dorsal fins that resemble the natural animal. (See Barbeau, 1950 and 1953; Duff *et al*, 1967; Stewart, 1979; Halpin, 1981).

Holm's great contribution to artists, teachers and enthusiasts of Northwest Coast art was a visual grammar to describe what they were making and seeing, as well as a rationale to bring them deeper into the art's aesthetic and meaning.

How can we enhance our appreciation of argillite sculpture?

The best way to appreciate this sculpture is to ask questions about what is before us. Encountering the sculpture means encountering the visual thoughts of another person, the artist. Begin by getting on the same level as the sculpture—literally. Recall that as he is carving, the artist shifts the stone in his hands as well as in his mind's eye; place yourself at eye-level with the sculpture. Look into the eyes of the images. Examine

6: Face of the dead hero on the back of *Lazy Son-in-law and the Wasgo Skin* by Robert Vogstad.

how one form relates to another. If you are able to, hold the piece in your hands; touch it and turn it.

Then begin to ask questions. If the artist isn't present, the piece itself will give you many answers or at least send you away trying to find them. The fun of discovery is entering into this dialogue. The value of encountering argillite sculpture comes from knowing we are on a journey, eyes open wide, seeking insight through sight.

One of your first questions may be about meaning. What story or portion of a story is the artist conveying? Look for visual clues. For example, on the back of Robert Vogstad's *Lazy Son-in-law and the Wasgo Skin* is a man's bearded face, eyes closed. Who is that man? In Marcel Russ's *Shaman Torturing a Witch*, the shaman is shown wearing an octopus on his head. What does that mean? The titles to both pieces give us our first clues as to what story or cultural event the artist is portraying.

The man's face below Wasgo's fin represents the person who has killed, then put on the skin, of Wasgo. Taking on the sea monster's supernatural powers, he brings whales to his starving village. Eventually, the man dies from these superhuman efforts. When the villagers cut open the dead Wasgo, the hero's face is revealed.

Octopus is a spirit helper of Haida shamans. Marcel has shown us that this is a shaman by enveloping the shaman's head in a half-mask, half-headdress made of an octopus's entire body.

27

7: Shaman wearing an Octopus mask in *Shaman Torturing a Witch* by Marcel Russ.

In looking at a sculpture, it is helpful to examine all parts of the piece. In apparently symmetrical forms, is there asymmetry? Looking at Donnie Edenshaw's *Panel Pipe*, we are drawn to the raven and seal figures at one end. Holding it, we discover Donnie has carved each side of the pipe's end differently.

On one side of the pipe, the raven's wing is collected against the seal's front flipper and the raven's tail is tucked under the bird's shoulder. On the reverse, Donnie has spread the raven's wing to embrace the little seal, with the foot of the raven under the bird's shoulder.

While parts of an animal's anatomy such as the shoulder or tail joints of a bird are usually shown as ovoids, we should immediately remember that ovoids may also be used to shape a head. When the ovoid is filled with a face, we may be looking at two things at once: a tail of a bird and a human head that gives us clues to the bird's supernatural identity by revealing the personification of the animal.

8: (upper facing) A lesson in asymmetry in design: the Raven and seal figures on the end of Donnie Edenshaw's panel pipe are portrayed differently on each side of the panel. On one side, Raven's wing touches the flipper of the seal. His tail is under the wing's shoulder.

9: (lower facing) On the reverse, Raven's wing is outstretched; his foot is under the wing's shoulder. Note the different treatment of the wing feathers.

10: (left) Supernatural face in the joint of Thunderbird's tail in *Thunderbird and Killer Whale* by Gary Minaker Russ. Note how the artist has overlapped the tail feathers.

"Transformation" is a key concept in Haida stories and arts. Many supernatural beings can alter their appearance between animal and human forms. In argillite art the act of transforming is portrayed in many ways. One way is to explicitly depict a limb or appendage shifting from one shape to another, as Gary Minaker Russ has done with his *Supernatural Man Who Married the Eagle King's Daughter*.

Another way to show the transformation process is to depict a human dancing in a mask. This is art imitating life, for that is exactly what happens in some Haida dances. Freddie Wilson's *Raven Dancer* is a good example. From one viewpoint, we know we are seeing a human in ceremonial regalia—cedar bark ring around the neck, blanket, apron, and mask—but from another, the dancer becomes the supernatural animal.

From this view, the Raven Dancer is human, shown with arms, human legs and hands, wearing a mask and a blanket over his shoulders.

From the opposite side, the man's blanket has become a bird's wings, back and tail. The dancer *is* Raven.

11: (above) A human foot is caught in the moment of transformation into an eagle's claw in Gary Minaker Russ's *Supernatural Man Who Married the Eagle King's Daughter.*

12: (below left) *Raven Dancer* by Freddie Wilson. On one side of the sculpture, the masked human dancer wears a ceremonial blanket, cedar bark neck ring and a dancing apron, and holds an axe.

13: (below right) On the reverse, the Raven Dancer's mask merges with a blanket that has transformed into the bird's wings and tail feathers.

Certain personality characteristics of the artists may find their way into their sculptures. Mike Brown and Darrell White can tease us with images when they think we may take ourselves too seriously in interpreting their sculpture. For example, Mike's frog pipe is filled with images of frogs exchanging tongues. We only have to imagine what will happen when the owner of this pipe places his mouth on the stem end and comes nose to nose with the frog whose tongue will lick the person's nose.

Haida humour is at its best when it comes as a surprise. When Darrell White carved a human face in the blowhole of a killer whale on an argillite pole, he seemed to be representing a conventional image: human faces often fill the ovoid of a whale's blowhole. But turning the pole to the back, we find the small male figure has pierced the pole, squeezing his head and arms through the gold-rimmed blowhole while leaving the rest of his body on the back of the pole.

14: (above) The stem end of Mike Brown's pipe. Theoretically the smoker's mouth would connect with the extended frog's tongue for a different kind of communication.

15: (below) Mike Brown's *Frog Pipe* depicts four frogs resting on the stem of a pipe. The bowl of the pipe is in the frog's head on the far right. The exchange of tongues symbolizes communication.

31

32

16: (above) On the *Legends of the Haida* crest pole, a small man emerges from the gold-rimmed blowhole of a large killer whale. The blowholes of killer whales are often depicted as ovoids with human faces. In this instance, artist Darrell White has extended the convention by creating a whole man squeezing himself out of the blowhole: head, shoulders and arms push against Killer Whale's forehead.

17: (left) On the reverse side of the crest pole, the rest of the man's body struggles to push through the orca's blowhole.

18: (upper facing) Gary Minaker Russ creates a unique formline design that incorporates his initials.

19: (lower facing) Donnie Edenshaw incorporated images of his own palms into his sculpture *Shark Woman Dancing*.

Artists may introduce deeply personal elements that only they and their collector may know. When we discover these secrets, we truly come closer to the artists' thoughts. Rather than just signing the bottom of his sculptures with his name, Gary Minaker Russ devised a formline image of his initials that fits into an inner ovoid that is part of his unique stylistic signature.

Donnie Edenshaw felt so personally attached to his *Shark Woman Dancing* sculpture that he carved the image of his own palms on her hands so that people viewing the piece would see his hand in its creation.

Argillite sculpture is shaped by hands and minds. We have an obligation to recognize that process, and we will be rewarded with deeper understanding and enjoyment of Haida art and culture when we bring our minds to the task. Argillite is good to see and good to think.

BREATH INTO STONE:
Creating *Gunarhnesemgyet*

The raw stone has spoken to Cooper Wilson: there is a great supernatural killer whale inside this large, rough argillite block that measures 40 centimetres in height. The whale has stolen the wife of Gunarhnesemgyet and holds her in its mouth. The husband, intent on rescuing his wife from the orca, rides the whale's back, holding on to the dorsal fin with all his might. It is a story this Haida artist knows well, but the stone's shape requires careful thought. After weeks of examining the argillite, Cooper is ready to carve.

Waiting for the stone to reveal what is inside is an experience that many argillite carvers describe; few are willing to impose a design on the stone. The stone will tell them what it wants to be. Sometimes that happens quickly, other times it takes weeks, months, or even years for the inspiring vision to materialize.

20: October 1. Cooper Wilson has made exploratory cuts on a large chunk of argillite that has a vein of minerals running down one side.

21: The reverse side of the stone shows a deep fissure that Cooper must consider as he works out his carving plan.

October 1: Cooper's piece of argillite has come from the earth encrusted with other minerals. It's a complication argillite artists usually encounter and have to consider carefully, for until they remove the outer crust of deposits, the true shape of the stone is not apparent. Some artists, rather than sacrifice a large portion of the rock, will accept some minor flaws or even incorporate them into the design. Cooper has sawn away parts of the rock around the dorsal fin and begun filing away the rusty-coloured mineral layer with a large steel rasp. The work goes slowly; like all argillite carvers, Cooper watches for flaws and is prudently vigilant for fractures.

Filling and sanding minute cracks is an ongoing task for all argillite sculptors. It is not unheard of for an entire chunk of stone to suddenly flake off the sculpture, an event that brings a host of problems and artistic decisions the artist is forced to make before continuing. Sometimes a broken sculpture will be shelved for weeks while the artist develops a new concept.

22: October 1. Detail showing rasp marks.

23: Detail showing knife and chisel marks.

October 4: Within a few days Cooper's sculpture has begun to take shape. He has roughed out the whale's nose and mouth. After pencilling in the shape of the man's bent leg behind the whale's dorsal fin (left photo), he has used a large gouge to define it further. Thus far, the argillite seems sound to the artist, free of major fractures and cracks.

There are still mineral deposits to remove from the sides of the argillite, which Cooper does carefully, shaving away millimetre by millimetre with gouges and knives, unwilling to waste any of the stone. Removing the deposits will alter the shape of the piece, and possibly affect the design. Argillite artists meticulously plan sizeable cuts so that any large pieces that are removed whole can be saved for other uses such as pendants or smaller sculptures.

24: October 4. Cooper has begun to rough out the whale's nose and Gunarhnesemgyet's bent legs.

25: Deep gouges in the stone indicate where Killer Whale's tail will be.

October 7: Using ever finer flat and round files, then switching to knives and chisels, Cooper gives shape to Gunarhnesemgyet's arms and legs. He defines the killer whale's bifurcated tail so that it is wrapped along one side of the sea mammal's body (right photo). Cooper has begun carving the whale's mouth and the outer ovoid of the eye sockets. By undercutting the man's bent legs and arms with a blade, he renders them as more sculptural forms.

Implicit in Haida sculpture is formline design—the hallmark of Haida two- and three-dimensional art. Argillite sculptors must carefully consider each element in the piece, its positioning and how to make it relate to every other element. Most Haida carvers are sensitive to flow and balance in their own and other artists' sculptures, qualities they strive to incorporate into every piece they create.

26: October 7. Cooper gives shape to Gunarhnesemgyet's arms and legs.

27: October 8. The orca's bifurcated tail folds against one side of its body.

November 11: After a month of working on the sculpture, Cooper has removed the final vestiges of the mineral deposits, leaving behind a solid large block of fine argillite free of mineral veins and fracture lines. He has begun shaping the stone to his vision, working out the interrelationships between the forms, until he's confident of their placement. Then he's ready to introduce several abalone inlays into the sculpture. Cooper has placed formlines of the whale's face so that the eye ovoids and eyelid lines have revealed the correct locations to place the abalone for the eyeballs.

As he considers the shape of the man's body, Cooper makes decisions about how the head will appear. He's partially carved the man's face, but it occurs to him that it is too small for the rest of the body. There's more thinking needed to solve this aesthetic dilemma. At this juncture, Cooper is also thinking about the whale's mouth holding the woman and how he will bring his vision of her into the design. The man's right foot is still undeveloped; Cooper must make a decision: will it overlap or tuck under the whale's pectoral fin?

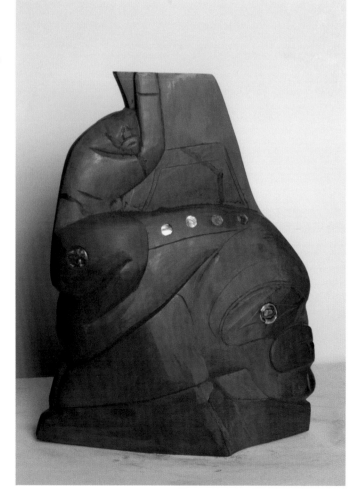

28: November 11. Cooper begins working out the interrelationships between the human and orca forms.

29: November 12. Abalone inlays are inserted at this time.

Haida carvers in argillite are continually thinking about the forms that shape their sculptures. They ask themselves what will fit, how will it fit, and what conventions they can adapt within their own individual styles. The artists continually consider the best way to exploit the stone's shape while honouring the image within, and at the same time, to best communicate the story to the people who will see their sculptures.

December 14: Cooper has incised the dorsal fin, pectoral fins, and parts of the man's body with formline elements and inlaid the man's shoulder, hip and ankle joints with abalone disks. He's decided to cover the man's right toes with the whale's pectoral fin. He has begun to refine the dorsal fin's shape and has carved the fingers on the man's left hand.

Cooper has chosen to separate the man's body from the whale's dorsal fin by carefully piercing the stone between them. This is a slow and delicate process, handled with fine blades. One slip or jolt and he will risk breaking the body off the orca's back. Cooper has found the inevitable tiny flaws in the stone and he's repaired them. With careful shaving and sanding, his repaired surfaces will be undetectable from the rest of the sculpture.

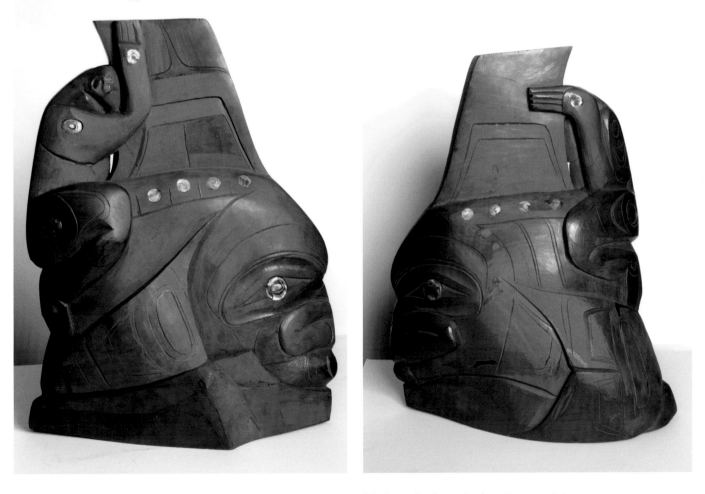

30: December 14. The formline design elements on the human and whale bodies have been further developed.

31: Cooper has begun to pierce the space between the man's body and the orca's dorsal fin.

Argillite artists thinly incise formlines as they develop the sculpture until they are sure the placement of the elements is correct. They may make the decision to obliterate or correct some lines by smoothly sanding the stone and redrawing elements until forms and lines satisfy their aesthetic sense. Their process of thinking and rethinking each element continually refines the sculpture, bringing their vision closer to the stone's intended form.

January 15: Cooper has been carving for more than three months and, at this stage, the major components of all three figures are evident. The finer points have become clearly visible: he has increasingly separated the man's body from the dorsal fin; deepened the separation of the pectoral fins from the sculpture's base; and added more definition to the ovoids, S-forms on the whale's body, and U-forms in the fins. He has developed ovoids around the man's joints that he previously inlaid with abalone.

Cooper has decided to leave enough argillite atop the man's shoulders to attach a separately carved head that he will glue to the larger piece. With

40

32: January 15. The kidnapped wife figure in the whale's mouth has been developed.

33: January 16. The separation between the man's chest and the dorsal fin is now wider.

skill borne of years of carving argillite, he will make the seam for this addition invisible. As the forms are still being refined, polishing is begun.

This stage of finishing and refining is tedious and takes weeks of shaving and scraping away minute layers of the argillite. It is, however, a stage that the most experienced artists endure, for they value the result: a smooth, skin-like finish to the sculpture that makes the stone images so life-like they appear to be breathing.

April 13: Cooper has finally solved the best way to depict the woman's inverted figure in the whale's mouth. He's decided to make the side of her skull appear parallel to the base of the sculpture, chin thrust forward. Her face is only visible from one side. Cooper has paid particular attention to her hair, which streams away from her head. Her arms are extended over the orca's lips and her hands clasped over its nostrils. Cooper has breathed reality into her struggle. The formline details of the whale's tail are finished as the polishing and refining of incised lines continues.

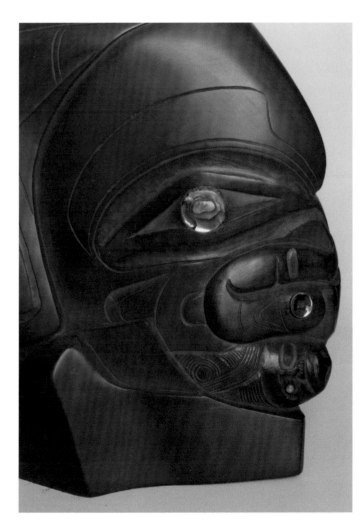

34: April 13. The artist has placed the woman's inverted figure in the whale's mouth and has begun carving details into her face and hair.

35: Cooper's formline design is more refined and the tool finishing and polishing have begun.

In details such as these, argillite artists can reveal their finest techniques: flawlessly incising parallel rows of ridged elements; making delicate crosshatching incisions in stone that are rhythmic and free of chips; tool-finishing surfaces that gleam as if they'd been sanded; and organically bending formline design around sculptural shapes to blend all aspects of two- and three-dimensional form.

April 18: It's taken six months for Cooper Wilson to carve the huge *Gunarhnesemgyet*. His argillite sculpture reveals the intensity of this dramatic scenario. The whale seems to vault and twist, trying to shake the hero from its back; the woman in Killer Whale's mouth struggles in terror. It's a good story, breathed into stone.

36: April 18. Cooper's powerful *Gunarhnesemgyet* sculpture is finished.

37: (facing) The stone seems to breathe, animating the dramatic story of the husband who rides the back of the supernatural killer whale that has kidnapped the man's wife.

COOPER WILSON

Building a legacy takes time, a strong will, and a massive amount of hard work. It also takes sensitivity and intelligence. Cooper Wilson is a legacy-builder—and he's doing it his way. This is not a break from his deep Haida heritage, but a vibrant response to the larger world which the Haida have always considered part of their own territory. Like his seafaring ancestors, Cooper has travelled widely, encountering other cultures, technologies and people head-on, learning from them as much as showing them what it means to be Haida.

Cooper Wilson's reach is far and impressive. Sending his argillite sculpture into cultures and landscapes well beyond his Haida Gwaii homeland, he teaches other people about the natural and supernatural life of the inhabitants of these beautiful islands. In his hands, a pod of killer whales swirl and mass with such fervour beneath the arc of a walrus tusk that they send their spirit images twisting and writhing up its ivory shaft. The orcas turn in his hand, their images sharpened by his chisel until they roll and leap in our mind. We recall, somewhere in our memories of this rain-soaked, misty landscape, seeing the whales cavorting in Masset Sound, and then the memory becomes more: a supernatural encounter of such intensity we swear we've been there too. Our fingers linger on the argillite base, our eyes trace along the ivory, unravelling orca forms.

38: Weighing nearly 100 pounds, this sculpture depicts two Raven stories from the time of Creation: how Raven stole a ball of light from his grandfather, Sky Chief, and Raven's discovery of the first men in a clamshell on the beach at Naikoon.

39: (lower facing) Opposite side of Cooper's Raven creation stories sculpture. On the right, Raven cradles the shell with its writhing human contents; his long beak rests on his wing feathers as he wonders what to do with this unusual bounty. In some stories, he sings a song to soothe the First People.

Part of Cooper Wilson's legacy resides in his children—four sons, three daughters, a son-in-law, and six grandchildren. The generosity of his time has enriched their lives and built the human side of his artistic legacy. Sons Donnie Edenshaw and Freddie Wilson, and son-in-law Sean Brennan, are fine argillite sculptors in their own right. As evidenced in international collections that hold their work, they reflect Cooper's teaching:

I taught them, not so much by formal lessons but by being around and doing my art for most of their lives. We learn most things—fishing, hunting, putting up food for the winter, and even creating art—by doing. We teach by showing how to do something, then letting the person do it for himself. They will make their own way, make their own legacies, but I'd like to think I helped them.

Cooper copies the method of his own training with his children. As a young man of 16, he returned to Old Masset from residential school and quickly became a regular at the Yeltatzie household. "Flossie Yeltatzie took me in," he recalls, "and I was exposed to a lot of artists hanging around there, carving argillite." His memory of those days remains crisp:

I remember looking at the dining room table covered with argillite carvings and pendants. One day I said to them, "How about letting me market

40, 41: (above) Cooper Wilson.

45

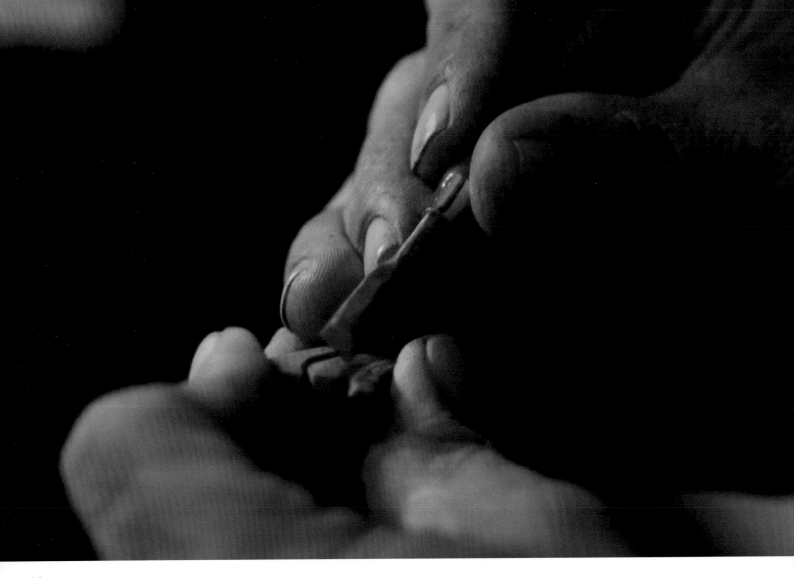

42: (above) Cooper uses a small chisel to incise details on a pendant.

43: (upper facing) One of Cooper Wilson's favourite themes is Raven Dancer. On one side, the dancer is seen from the back, his body cloaked in a button blanket with a raven crest. The blanket's design shows Raven's head in profile, crossing the shoulder ovoid on one of his flaring wings.

44: (lower facing) Viewed from the other side, there's a little surprise contained in this sculpture. While the dancer appears to be a human wearing a Raven mask and a dance apron with another Raven design, his feet and one hand appear to be bird-like claws. Is the dancer becoming Raven, or is Raven caught in the act of transformation into his human form?

these for you." I sold them to the continual rotation of workers at the armed forces base and at the hospital here in Masset. It wasn't long before I wanted to learn to carve myself. So when I was 17 I joined the artists sitting around the Yeltatzie table and they began to show me how to carve. They helped me make the tools I needed and showed me how to improve on my pieces. There was no one teacher or one special class, but the group encouraged me and started me on my way.

Sitting at the table, Cooper absorbed the techniques of artists such as Donald Edgars, Martin Williams, John and George Yeltatzie, Fred Davis, and Louis and Richard Widen (who are son-in-law Sean's uncle and father respectively). Their lessons inspired Cooper's artistic life and his vision for the future.

Part of Cooper Wilson's legacy resides in his vision for preserving Haida art and cultural heritage by re-creating the same kind of artistic community that fostered his own growth as an artist. In designing and building a 21st century Haida longhouse, he will fulfill his vision to make his house a community of cultural learners and practitioners.

The frame of the massive two-story cedar structure stands tall against the domed sky above Masset. Ravens flocked to its beams in the early days of construction, their very vocal presence signalling a triumph of one Haida Raven man's vision coming into reality. It is a house built with ingenious forethought, tough-mindedness, and patience. Ever-demanding patience.

Setting aside delicate chisels, scribers, and engravers used for shaping argillite, ivory, and silver, Cooper wields chain saws, routers, adzes, planers, and other logging tools. His hands peeled behemoth red cedars of their bark, then with the help of a son or son-in-law guided the horizontal blade of an Alaska sawmill across their massive lengths to produce 25-foot planks, four inches thick and 20 or more inches wide. The planks formed the frame and walls of the longhouse.

With continued patience, he had architects and engineers refine his plans for the inner structure of separate studios, performance spaces, and living quarters. Electronic systems for live web-casts of artists at work—carving, weaving, painting—are part of his vision for connecting the entire world with real-time views. He has designed a business plan for this century of Haida artists coming together in community, contributing to the preservation of Haida heritage through the traditional visual and performing arts and creating a springboard for Haida innovation and thought. The longhouse will be a place of intense activity, a place of contemplation and imagination, a place where legacies are born and encouraged. For Cooper Wilson, it is a living legacy.

Legacy building, Cooper will patiently explain, begins in his own hands and mind—literally—as his vision and ideas are hewn from this black stone. A master artist in wood, silver, ivory and a host of non-traditional sculpting media such as amber, Cooper says, "I keep coming back to argillite." The stone has become the source of his inspiration and his avocation. It connects with his spiritual energy. "My artwork is my spiritual side," he says. "It is the source of my beliefs and my strength. The ideas come to me and I am able to transform them into my art. I don't know if you've noticed, but Spirits run pretty strong here on the island."

It's hard not to notice.

Cooper doesn't waste time or argillite. The stone comes to his hands raw and dirty; the black dust clings to his skin and is embedded under his fingernails. He moves it, looks at it, listens for what the stone has to say. Its shape suggests a form, what he describes as a "body mass." Then he begins carving. It's a long process of continually refining and shaping; new forms may evolve and change as the piece progresses. "All the time I'm carving," he says, "I don't let the purpose of working large go to waste. It's meant to be big, massive, so I don't want to take away too much stone."

First the large knives, gouges, and files come out. He continually moves the stone, blowing away the fine argillite dust with each

47

stroke. The black grains soon cover his hands, his arms, his clothing, and any horizontal surface within a two-foot radius. The grating of his rasp against the argillite is punctuated by the intermittent sound of Cooper blowing away the dust—it's as if he's breathing life into its inert form. As he works, he describes being engaged with the stone: "always thinking, deciding about the forms and their relationships to one another." How the work progresses, he says candidly, "depends on the argillite."

Inspiration comes from nature: first from the shape itself, then from the surrounding environment. One day, for example, Cooper was struggling with the image of Raven holding the sun in his beak when one of the sleek black birds landed not far from where he was carving outside his studio. The raven playfully began tossing a small red ball, holding it in his beak for long periods of time. "It was like he was modelling for me, showing me how I should carve the beak, turn the head just so, have a certain look in the eye. He did that for the longest time. I learned a lot about Raven that day."

Sometimes, he says, the stone gives him sudden jolts: surprises like cracks or even the flaking off of an entire piece. "When that happens," Cooper smiles, "it's almost as if the piece is telling me that it's not done yet and I have to keep carving. Funny thing is, the sculpture ends up being shaped more as it should be."

45: (facing) Cooper carves a large walrus tusk in his trailer studio. Around this table several young carvers have gathered to learn from Cooper and from each other. In the foreground is a massive argillite tableau of vaulting killer whales. The tusk he is carving rests on the deer antlers inserted into this argillite base.

46: (above) *Eagle and Salmon.* Small, exquisite, yet monumental, this sculpture of Eagle with a salmon in its talons reflects the Haida idea of *Yah'guudang*—respect for all living things. This successful hunter soars into the sky carrying a salmon (*tsiin*). These fish are integral to all life on Haida Gwaii, enabling human and eagle populations to flourish. Eagle's head and tail are carved from a walrus tusk. The salmon, also carved from ivory, is visible from the front.

Sometimes, I think I'm just about finished. That's when I go really slowly. It's almost like I can see the end coming and I don't want it to be over. Sometimes that's when a really dramatic "accident" will happen. Something cracks, or flakes, or just falls away. That's an almost natural event—or supernatural. It's like my ancestors are speaking, saying, "Hey! You're not done yet!" It's spiritual guidance. I love it!

Eventually, though, the pieces are finished. "And then," he says, "they're gone. I have some photographs of my pieces; some are only mental images of what I've done, and some I forget." The forgotten and those committed to memory have something in common: they carry the breath of the carver. The images themselves seem to breathe.

Cooper's style is best described as monumental. Not only does he like "working big", but his images boldly fill spaces with movement and narrative. Raven is portrayed grasping the sun, stealthily exiting Sky Chief's house, and ready to soar into the sky with his stolen treasure. Cooper's killer whales don't simply breach the water's surface, they vault and cavort. In another huge argillite sculpture, Gunarh, the great hunter, rides the dorsal fin of a supernatural killer whale chief or *sga'na* with as much terror as determination. Sga'na, rising to the surface, grasps the hunter's kidnapped wife in his mouth and attempts to shake Gunarh free. The breathing stone compels the viewer to engage, to glimpse the fury of a supernatural encounter, and to feel the clash of wills.

In describing his own style, Cooper speaks of designs that "flow." He values the way designs fit together, one form influencing the next. At the same time he strives for "simple and to-the-point images that will capture people's minds and imaginations."

His message is always about being Haida:

I work in a unique Haida stone, and my images come from our songs and stories, from our culture and our landscape. Being Haida is something of a double-edged sword. Sometimes it's a big chore keeping things in balance, like Haida pride and being from the right lineage. I never feel discouraged, though. I come from a big family and I have a big family of my own. I'm building my own proud legacy.

I am a Raven from kuna 'laanaas, from the Tow Hill area. My mother was of the Raven clan. She died when I was young, so my grandmother and grandfather along with my dad raised me. My uncle was Alan Wilson. They taught me about food gathering and living off the land. My daughters, my sons, and my son-in-law: we're all Haida artists making our mark. Right now, my job is to take care of my legacy.

Cooper eschews labels for the artists of Haida Gwaii. Rather than speak of "traditional" or "contemporary" Haida arts, he prefers to deal in ideas that spring from being Haida. "There are too many labels," he observes:

*They've never been our labels. Just think back 200 years ago when Haida
artists were making all this beautiful art — what were they calling it then?
Scholars and their new words. They describe something as "traditional"
when they mean "old." The old artists were hard working and smart people.
They were working in response to the changing world around them, not just
repeating the same images over and over again. The culture was always
growing and changing, and they changed with it. That's the way I work: hard
and smart. I value my past heritage, but I also live in this century.*

Cooper Wilson is a legacy builder, working hard and smart,
informing the world about what it means to live as a Haida artist
through monumental works that reveal the intricate dance of the natural
and supernatural. Filled with character and meaning, Cooper's sculptures leave his hands, leave Haida Gwaii, but carry with them the breath
of insight and integrity. For Cooper Wilson, they are living testimony to
his work and to his vision.

47: *Raven with a Broken Beak.* Familiar with the
cycle of Raven stories, Cooper chose to illustrate a
particularly vivid story about how Raven, ever greedy,
decided to trick an old blind fisherman by stealing
his bait. Diving under the ocean, he pulled on the
man's line to free a tender morsel. Believing he'd
hooked a huge halibut, the man yanked the hook,
snagging Raven's beak and pulling it off his face.
Fastening the beak to the outside of his longhouse,
he shamed the notorious trickster. Eventually, under
the cover of night, Raven retrieved his beak and
re-attached it to his face, though imperfectly, for the
beak kept falling off, exposing his human persona.

DONNIE EDENSHAW
Gaju Xial

Raven moves cautiously around the beach at Naikoon. Hopping, dodging. Head tilting from side to side, one eye glances skyward, the other scours the wet sand left by the retreating tide for tantalizing bits of seafood. Raven's long, sharp beak clatters open and shut; clicking sounds vibrate from his thick dark throat. As the sun sets behind Tow Hill, a song moves through his body, drumming ever present in his ears. This raven appears bird-like, but his body is entirely human—a visual signal that this is no ordinary raven, but a supernatural being.

Donnie Edenshaw dances as Raven, the principle cultural hero of many Northwest Coast nations. For the Haida, Raven is credited with finding the first people at the dawn of time and bringing them many essential gifts such as the sun and the moon. Usually he acts not from some noble or magnanimous obligation to benefit humankind, but from his own persistent notions of self-gratification. A supernatural being who can transform himself into many plant and animal forms—from a spruce needle to a human baby—Raven is also a trickster, a voracious being, continually seeking satisfaction for his gastronomic and sexual appetites.

When Donnie Edenshaw portrays Raven in his art, he's cognizant of these complex ideas. His artistic expressions are driven by his intimate knowledge of the Haida dances, songs and stories that surround him.

Everything he creates as a visual or performing artist is his personal and cultural testimony to a whole constellation of visual and linguistic realities that have culminated following centuries of Haida thought and life.

At age three, Donnie Edenshaw, whose Haida name is *Gaju Xial*, meaning "Song and Dance Man", joined Claude Davidson's K'a.adsnee Dancers, a Haida group that performed in traditional dress with carved wooden masks. Donnie fondly remembers the dance classes in the Davidson home:

Those were good times. I was so young, but we did a lot of travelling with the K'a.adsnee Dancers. We even went to Expo 86. By that time I'd learned pretty much all of the songs from Claude and from my uncle Guujaaw. At first I sang the words phonetically, without knowing their meaning, and it wasn't until a lot later that I learned the actual Haida words and their English translations. My uncle Vernon Williams, who makes awesome cedar flutes, taught me some of his own Haida compositions.

By the time he was 10, Donnie decided to make his own art. He began by drawing pictures of his father's argillite pendants. "There were so many pieces that I wanted to carve," he says, "and argillite seemed to be the easiest for me." Much later, after mastering argillite sculpture, Donnie would turn to carving wood and ivory, and tried his hand at gold and silver. The credit for fostering his artistic skills rests firmly with his mother, Brenda Edenshaw, and his father, Cooper Wilson:

I'm glad both my parents are Haida. My mother and father kept me going. They taught me the real stuff and supported me doing art. They kept it fun, but they also impressed upon me that carving would be something useful in my life.

When I was a teen, carving gave me a reason to be home, a reason to develop as an artist. These were valuable lessons and because of them I am a carver, a singer, and a dancer.

These talents developed early in Donnie's life and are reflected in his poise and ease of performing in front of people. Sarah Davidson recalls that at the memorial potlatch for his grandfather, Lee Edenshaw, Donnie, then just 12 years old, stood up and gave a moving speech that had those attending alternately laughing and crying. "It was funny and serious at the same time," she recalls. "There was this little person speaking from his heart—it was impressive and the elders liked it."

By the time he was 14, Donnie began selling argillite pendants and little sculptures. Not content to repeat the same images and forms in argillite, he began looking at other carvers' work in Haida Gwaii, in books, and in museums. Everywhere he travelled he picked up new ideas and learned new artistic expressions in sculpture. At age 16, he began living by himself in a house provided by his father:

48: (facing) Donnie Edenshaw dances on the beach at Naikoon, where Raven found the first men in a clam shell. His mask has a moveable lower beak that he controls with hidden strings.

49: (above) Donnie's Haida name, *Gaju Xial*, means "Song and Dance Man."

I stayed home a lot and some of the other guys my age hung out with me. Guys like Shaun Edgars. I used to call him "Taco." I grew up with him my whole life. Now our kids are growing up together.

They were learning to carve just as I was. Sometimes they'd ask me to teach them. It's hard to teach other people to carve just because I don't know how to put it into words. So I taught them as my father taught me: learn by doing. No one taught me how to carve an ovoid; I had to watch others.

I had to get used to people looking over my shoulders, watching, just as I looked over the shoulders of other Haida carvers.

We're taught to know what we know; we're taught to teach what we know.

In Donnie's home village of Old Masset, prominent Haida artist and teacher Christian White started an apprenticeship program that Donnie attended as part of his interest in further refining his artistic skills and appreciation of the art market. Nevertheless, to this day Cooper remains the most powerful artistic influence in Donnie's life. Frequently, he can be found carving with his brother Freddie Wilson and his brother-in-law Sean Brennan in Cooper's trailer studio.

Donnie's father encouraged him to develop his own style, to be continually alert to possible stylistic changes that would take his art to a new level:

There are so many different artists that I've idolized, especially carvers in wood and argillite. I experiment a lot in wood, but my own argillite style seems to stay the same, though my dad encourages experimenting with different forms and finishes. I look at what he does — as well as other carvers like Martin Williams — and I always try to improve my work. My dad always told me, "Don't try to be better than someone else, just try to be better than yourself."

Mostly, I want to be satisfied with my work. If I want people to like my work, I want to like it first.

Donnie approaches a raw chunk of argillite without preconceived notions of what the finished sculpture will look like. Like many argillite sculptors, once he gets an idea, he will examine the stone for flaws, cracks and natural grain, and sometimes scribe a few lines. Then there's more time spent gazing at the stone's raw form, turning it physically and in his mind. "The stone talks to you — shows you what it should be," he says. "Then you do what it tells you. It's always different from what you expect."

He's tried other methods. He's tried working from sketches. ("It's easier just drawing right on the piece.") He's also tried to find a stone shape that fits his idea for a sculpture. These methods don't work for him. "The ideas are in the piece, in the stone; you can't just tell the stone what to be." He even tried making clay models. ("For all the time it takes to do that, you may as well carve," he says dismissively.) Carving in argillite is different from carving in wood, Donnie maintains, because the physical characteristics of the two materials are so different, and these dictate the size, form and techniques the artist can employ. In particular, with argillite, the shape and size of the stone varies from piece to piece. Carving in argillite means starting with the block of stone, then removing excess material to achieve form.

Donnie's process for carving the monumental *Supernatural Eagle with Salmon* began with hiking up Slatechuck to saw raw argillite out of the mountainside. The argillite weighed over 80 pounds; it was the biggest single piece he'd ever collected, and the biggest that he'd ever carved. "Until recently," he says, "we weren't able to take out such a large piece because in years past someone tried to dynamite the mountain. Even if a large slab was taken out, it was full of fractures — probably from the shock waves and then the moisture that went through the mountain. It doesn't take much to crack argillite."

Getting the stone down the steep mountain was a challenge on the steep wet slopes. More than once he fell on his back in the mud, his heavy stone-filled backpack beneath him: "You don't really appreciate argillite until you've made that big hike," he says. "Coming down with a full pack is OK for the first little while — you're real glad to have all that stone — but suddenly you reach a point and think, 'I've got another three hours to go!'"

55

50: (facing) *Raven Panel Pipe* reveals a complex scenario of Haida creatures fashioned around a pipe form. Raven's beak touches the bowl of the pipe; the stem is covered with supernatural figures including Dragonfly with its long proboscis and double cross-hatched wings. This form of argillite panel carving was popular in the early 19th century. The pipe rests in front of a traditionally woven cedar bark hat.

51: (above) *Supernatural Eagle and Salmon.* (detail). Donnie carved the head of Eagle from a whale tooth and inlaid it into the argillite body of the great bird.

52: (facing) *Supernatural Eagle and Salmon.*

53: (above) The back of *Supernatural Eagle and Salmon* reveals that this is a supernatural eagle because it has a human face in the ovoid that is the bird's tail joint. The face, seen upside down, has the nose of a transformer. In her lip is a large labret, indicating that the human form of this Eagle is a high ranking and wealthy female. The teeth of the transforming image are made from opercula.

The argillite sat in his studio for weeks before he began to carve. He would look at it one day, get a few ideas—"raw argillite always looks like *something*," he says—then the black stone would seem to change, giving him a different idea of what it wanted to be and how it should look. From the first, he thought he saw Eagle in the stone, but he found that the stone was so big that when he tried to visualize that image, the stone's internal shape shifted again to resemble other forms. "Sometimes the stone just doesn't want to be what you want it to be," he explains. "I remember what I first saw in the stone, what I visualized, but that's not how it came out."

Eventually Eagle did emerge from the argillite. Mighty wings seem to stretch from the stone; a tail bearing the transformer's face—a human-like face with a nose that curves into the mouth—supports the massive body. The supernatural bird triumphantly sinks his claws into a stunned salmon. Defiantly, the eagle arches his long neck forward, white feathers stretched smooth, beak strongly down-turned, eyes flashing.

Once the form was established, Donnie began to visualize the details. Eagle's head, white in the natural world of bald eagles, was shaped from a whale's tooth. Carving the tooth and fitting it into the bird's argillite body presented its own problems, but the resulting feathered skull and beak honoured the natural animal's grace and noble countenance. Mammoth ivory formed the great salmon's fins; opercula (natural shell-like white ovals that are the "trap doors" or lids of red turban snails) were inlaid into the mouth of the transformation face on Eagle's tail. Abalone inlays in eyes plus the labret on the tail face as well as in the wings enhance the monumental piece by bringing light to the sleek dark stone. The finishing touch, however, was achieved by painstakingly carving each scale on the salmon and each feather on the bird's inner and outer wings, a process that took weeks. After nine months, the sculpture was finished.

Soon after the Eagle left his hands it was sold to a Canadian collector. "I always wonder where my stuff is," Donnie muses:

I wish I had a way to track my pieces down, to see them again. After working so hard on them for so many months, I get attached to them, and I miss them when they're gone. After nine months of carving a single piece, I can still feel the piece in my hands; there's something in every piece that you never forget, some part of you. That's why I carved the image of my own hands on the sculpture of Shark Woman Dancing. *I wanted the new owner to see my hands when he holds the sculpture—to be reminded that this piece came from my hands into his.*

Sometimes, Donnie's pieces don't leave his studio exactly when he anticipates they will. His wife, Beverly, who often accompanies him singing and dancing, usually sees the pieces when they're almost complete. Solicited or not, she may offer a critique based on her own sensibilities as a visual artist. He laughs when he describes the scene:

58

54: (above) *Shark Woman Dancing*. Viewed from the back, Shark Woman's headdress is literally depicted as a shark, while her ceremonial button blanket bears a two-dimensional shark design.

55: (facing) *Shark Woman Dancing* tells the story of a small supernatural female shark that was trapped in a tidal pool in Old Masset. The receding tide would have threatened her life, but a Haida man saved her by releasing her back into the ocean. In gratitude, Shark Woman gave a song and dance to the man, allowing him to use her image as a personal crest. Small sharks inhabiting waters off Haida Gwaii are known as a dogfish; Shark is sometimes called "Mother of Dogfish".

There have been times when Bev will just look at what I've carved and say, "Do you think you're done?" or even worse, "Are you going to sell it like that?" Just when I think I am done and ready to sell the piece. She's almost always right, though, and I have a few more hours of carving ahead of me before she agrees it's finished. She's got a good eye.

Now a father of two girls, Mya and Sarah, Donnie feels a strong obligation to his family's future. He playfully concedes that "it is fun having them around because they don't ask too many questions while I'm working that will take me out of the zone." He considers their interest in the arts as part of his obligation to teach them; it is an aspect of the larger responsibility he feels to contribute to Haida culture.

For a period, he concentrated on carving and found little time for singing and dancing. "The *naaniis* got after me for neglecting that part of my life, so I began singing again. They really supported me then." In 1995–96 he brought together 80 dancers of all ages from Old Masset and formed the White Sandy Beach Dancers, *Aaw Xaade Kyeles:*

People twice my age began teaching the group. I was never comfortable teaching or speaking, so anything I have to say I sing — from congratulations to joy or to sorrow — singing is my expression just the way carving is my therapy for expressing when I'm happy, angry or whatever feelings I have.

But what I also learned was that beyond my art, my role as a Haida artist is important. I tried to walk away from part of that role, but found that I couldn't take singing and dancing for granted any more than I could take carving and my art for granted. As a Haida artist I have a responsibility to my family and to my nation.

Because of my art, I've seen and touched things in many different cultures. They are valued things in the world. I want people to think that way about my culture, about Haida Gwaii.

Donnie Edenshaw, a member of the Raven clan of Old Masset in Haida Gwaii, continues to look to the future of his island home with optimism. Though Aaw Xaade Kyeles has disbanded for the time being, he's confident that another group will happen in the near future, perhaps encouraged by the longhouse being built by his father, Cooper Wilson.

There's something about being Haida. By comparison to other nations, a lot of people know about us. While other people have adopted Haida Gwaii as home, I've lived here all my life. All I do — the art, dancing and singing — is what I have to do. It's a responsibility to show people what we have. Just as I continue to learn about my culture — studying Haida arts and culture, visiting ancient village sites such as Naden Harbour, Kung, Yan, Kiusta and Dadens — I have to teach others.

This is the first step: that is, everything I have done so far.

The next step is my father's longhouse. It will change our family's lives. My role is to help preserve Haida culture. With this longhouse standing there will be a place for me and my family to pass on a living Haida culture to our children. The longhouse will be one more place where Haida culture enjoys a big revival through our songs, dances and arts.

A devoted environmentalist and promoter of Haida culture, Donnie looks forward to the day that great longhouses will line Haida Gwaii beaches as they did more than a century ago. He won't be a passive observer when this day comes, however; he sees his role as active, vital, and innovative. Through his argillite sculpture as well as his gifts in other visual and performing arts, Donnie Edenshaw is making sure that the world will continue to know and care about the people of Haida Gwaii.

56: Donnie Edenshaw is passing on his knowledge of Haida culture to his daughters Mya (left) and Sarah.

FREDDIE WILSON

In his studio, a radio blares with the Phoenix-Raptors game. Freddie Wilson has shed his expensive hip-hop clothes—designer jeans, elaborate hoodie, and the newest baseball cap—opting instead for old jeans and a sweatshirt black with argillite dust. Head bent, he works steadily, repeatedly pushing the fine graving tool through the black stone, refining the curve of an orca's fin, finessing the cross-hatching in a split-U form. Rhythmically he blows dust from the edge of his chisel. The fine black powder sticks to his hands, and smudges his cheek. With eyes as dark as if made of argillite itself, he examines every stroke he makes against the fine-grained stone, cutting and scraping for a few minutes, then turning the piece to see where his next cut will be.

This young Haida is part of the fastest growing First Nations demographic: urban youth. For part of the year he resides in Vancouver, savouring all that this vibrant setting has to offer. "Living in the city

keeps me closer to the art markets, the galleries and collectors," he confides. It also keeps him closer to the things he and other twenty-somethings value: the music, nightlife, shopping, and friends who share his enthusiasms for art, restaurants, basketball, and hip-hop tunes.

By contrast, the sculptures he produces come from a different, deeply Haida sensibility. Born in Queen Charlotte City into the Raven clan from the village of *q'una 'llnagaay* (Skedans) in Gwaii Haanas (South Morsesby) in Haida Gwaii, he grew up in Old Masset with his father, Cooper Wilson, and his mother, Brenda Edenshaw. One of nine children in his extended family, Freddie learned about Haida art by being surrounded by it:

When I was living with my father, I was pretty much living with the art all the time. In the beginning, my dad would always be there to help me if I got stuck. When I first started carving, he'd square off a piece of argillite, then give it to me, and I'd take over with carving the designs. Sometimes he'd do the reverse — have me do the initial block and then he'd start the piece and take me through the many different steps such as where to make the first cut, then what the second cut should be, and so on. I learned how to start a piece and how to finish it. Step-by-step he's taught me different variations in the whole process.

Even though he began carving argillite in his late teens — his first piece was a small crest pole — Freddie has achieved advanced design capabilities while refining his own stylistic signature. The resulting success was swift — galleries in Haida Gwaii, Vancouver, and Calgary began featuring his sculptures. His pieces sold quickly and for handsome prices.

Freddie's initial motivation for taking up art was financial. "I like the money," he says candidly. "I looked at working for a whole summer landscaping and earning only $1200 and compared that with the thousands of dollars my dad and brother Donnie earned carving argillite — it wasn't difficult to choose." The difference between creating art and working at a job made an impression on him:

I found argillite carving gave me all I was looking for — it was relaxing, it gave me a sense of freedom, and I could be acknowledged for my work.

I did four paintings for Sarah's gallery and realized how much money was to be made and the joy my art brought to the people buying my art, so I decided to start carving again and that was when I did my first argillite totem pole.

I wasn't great at it at first. I could see stuff I could have done better in each piece, and then I'd try to do it in my next piece.

Without slavishly copying old argillite sculptures, he was nonetheless inspired by one such piece, a large bear bowl carved from a single piece of argillite. The original, in the Glenbow Museum, was carved

63

57: (facing) *Double-Finned Killer Whale* represents a supernatural orca that is a prominent crest of the Raven clans. Orcas are often depicted with human faces peering out of or calling from the blowhole. This crest figure belongs to the *Yahku Láanaas* Raven clan.

58: (above) Freddie carving his *Double-Finned Killer Whale.*

by an anonymous Haida artist in the early years of the "third period" (1865-1910), and was featured in the book *Pipes That Won't Smoke; Coal That Won't Burn*. Similar bear bowls are found in other collections including the Museum of Anthropology at UBC, the Tacoma Museum of Fine Art, the Ipswich Museum in England, Chicago's Field Museum, and the Vancouver City Museum. At least two of the argillite bear bowls are attributed to Charles Edenshaw, one of the master artists from the past whom Freddie admires the most.

Freddie was excited about the bowl's size, the integral designs on its sides and back, and the strength of the overall form. Working with a sizable chunk of argillite, he made his own contribution to the many other bear bowls that paid homage to Edenshaw's 19th century bowl. Carving the massive piece with its elaborate configuration and multiple inlays was a challenge in itself, but Freddie had a deeper reason for attempting the bear bowl:

I liked the bowl because it's simple — but it's not actually. The faces in the paws and the ears are complicated and intricate. It took a lot of thinking and a lot of work to get it right.

I'm into doing more extravagant stuff like this bear bowl, doing sculptures that other people aren't doing. I want to try to do sculpture that's unique and the bear bowl helped teach me how I could do that. Right now, I'm doing my third raven rattle, my third, and I'm still learning new things.

When my art leaves my hands I sometimes imagine where it could be—how is it being displayed? In the end, I guess, it doesn't matter just as long as it's being appreciated and where others can see it and get something out of it.

Freddie's argillite sculptures are inspired almost as much by popular culture as by the history of visual ideas in argillite sculpture. He demonstrates versatility in seeing beyond what is "traditional" or conventional, and this inspires him to think in unconventional ways. One month he finished carving a supernatural double-finned killer whale, and then in the next he found tremendous satisfaction in fashioning a miniature argillite skateboard with trade-bead wheels for a friend. He spent dozens of hours carving an argillite version of a traditional kerfed box with a lid depicting Raven discovering humans in a clamshell, then took equal delight in another piece, a non-Haida image of a Chinese flying dragon with ivory teeth and a red catlinite tongue wrapped around the lid of a tiny argillite jewellery box, that he carved for different friend.

65

59: (facing) *Bear Bowl* is a replica of several 19th century argillite bowls done by different Haida masters. This particular bowl is modelled after one in the Glenbow Museum, though Freddie has put his own interpretations in the details.

60: Freddie's traditional *Bear Bowl* rests beside a small argillite skateboard with trade bead wheels carved as a gift for a friend.

This straddling of different Haida and non-Haida cultures through his carving in argillite is Freddie's direct link to Haida master artists of the last two centuries who thoughtfully and enthusiastically did the same thing. One has only to remember that between 1830-1865 — the "second period" in Haida argillite sculpture — artists created panel pipes with depictions of Euro-American sailors, women, architecture, and animals. Suddenly skateboards and Chinese dragons don't seem far-fetched subjects for argillite sculpture.

Freddie is constantly exploring the movement of massive forms. Sculptures of Raven dancers reveal the moment of transformation between the human dancer and Raven; supernatural double-finned Killer Whale arcs through the spray above the waves. Freddie describes his carving style as simply a balancing of form and line:

I like to include intricate detail, fill out everything in the sculpture, but at the same time keep it all balanced with not too much going on in one spot. For example, I like to do inlays of mastodon ivory and abalone, but they have to relate to the overall design and balance of the forms.

Most of my work doesn't come from a particular inspiration. I just hold the piece in my hands and start making some initial cuts. It's not always what I expect, though. Sometimes the stone changes my mind. Like this raven rattle. I started out thinking I'd cut the argillite into four pieces to be four poles, then after a few cuts, it just showed me it wanted to be a rattle.

Lately, most of my work is pure design; there aren't many stories behind what I do. Like the panel I carved recently. It started with Raven and then I went with the crests that are supposed to go with Raven and whatever looked like it should be there.

Primarily influenced by his father, Cooper Wilson, Freddie has also been inspired by other artists he greatly admires, such as his brother Donnie Edenshaw, Ben Davidson, Christian White, Jim Hart, Gwaai Edenshaw, and his uncle Guujaaw. Eagerly, he has learned valuable lessons from all of them. He acknowledges receiving special encouragement in his growing art career from gallery owner Sarah Hillis Davidson in Old Masset.

His goals include spending more time on design and expanding his repertoire of media to include wood, serigraphs and jewellery. "Although I love argillite, there's more money to be made if I expand into other design areas," he says confidently. In that respect, he's following the lead of his friends the Cree/Tsimshian artist Philip Gray and Haida artist Jay Simeon:

They work in other media — silver, gold and wood, for example — because people aren't always going to want to buy argillite exclusively. In growing my business I have to consider my growth as an artist moving into future market-

67

61: (facing upper left) *Raven Dancer* from one side shows the figure as the supernatural bird.

62: (facing upper right) The front of *Raven Dancer* depicts the human figure in ceremonial dress.

63: (facing lower) *Dancing Raven.* This image of a Raven Dancer carries a speaker's stick crowned with an ivory double-finned killer whale. Under his beak, the raven holds a copper, a symbol of chiefly rank and great wealth.

places. Working in gold appeals to me — someday I'd like to make myself a big pendant — but it's also a smart direction for me.

Working smart, working hard. Freddie Wilson is a young man with plans for the future. In a very short time, he's found his vocation and his avocation:

Now I mostly find myself carving eight to 13 hours a day — two main pieces at a time. I have come a long way in the last few years, and I only hope to get better.

I take pride in what I do. I try to keep the bar raised as high as all the artists before me did. At the same time, I don't want to live off the Haida name — people want good quality work and that's what I aim to do.

64: Freddie's argillite panel depicts a multitude of Haida figures who animate many traditional stories. From left to right: Raven, Frog, Bear, human, Killer Whale, Gunarh riding Killer Whale Chief, and Raven.

Looking beyond the dollars and the personal recognition, Freddie sees his argillite art as contributing to keeping Haida art traditions alive. He finds new inspiration in talking with elders, reading books, and studying the work of the Haida master artists from the last two centuries. Understanding the uniqueness of his heritage, and deeply respectful of the master artists from the past, Freddie Wilson is a 21st century Haida man with an eye to the future. "I'll always think of myself as an argillite carver. The thing is, I always know I'm going to be better tomorrow than I am today."

SEAN BRENNAN
Nunghlkayass

As traditional Haida songs and stories filter through his consciousness, Sean Brennan carves subtle details into the black stone. Heritage is foremost in Sean's mind as the argillite crest pole slowly takes shape in his hands. The pole is complex, intricate in form and meaning. His concentration unbroken, Sean focuses on each image, calculating the amount of argillite yet to be removed. The chisel shaves a micro-millimetre from a fin, barely strokes the outer ovoid on a wing, and smoothes a beak. He pauses, blows dust from where he's been working, and looks at the intertwined figures in his hands. His gaze is focused, intent.

One form flows into another, yet the animal crests are distinct, elegant. They honour individuals and families from the past, echoing certain features of the carved red cedar poles created by other Haida master artists. Sean's pole is not a copy or a mere compilation of traditional Haida images. It is a contemplation of himself as a Haida artist as he views his own life within a rich cultural and historical setting.

The stacked images on a pole represent family crests. On Sean's pole, they emerge with balanced grace. At the top, two watchmen or *skil* flank Killer Whale, who thrusts his head between a large raven's ears. His tall dorsal fin is poised between the watchmen's chiefly hats, each crowned with four potlatch rings. The basketry hat cylinders, also called skil, each symbolize a potlatch the owner has given, thus indicating his or her prestigious social standing. In Haida tradition, only the greatest chiefs had three watchmen at the top of their poles. Sean has created an innovation on this visual symbol, in effect using supernatural Killer Whale as the third watchman and completing the emblem of a high-ranking person.

Raven dominates the centre of the pole, his long straight beak thrust above the supernatural bear who married a woman and fathered her half-human, half-bear offspring. His wings envelop Bear Father's ears and the side of his head like a headdress. Beneath his great curled nostrils, Bear Father's wide lips gently grip a bear cub. The cub's protruding tongue is clasped in the hands of an upside-down human figure, Bear Mother in her human form. Tucked under Raven's chin and resting on Bear's head, barely visible, is another tiny bear cub.

On the table beside Sean is an argillite sculpture from his father's hands. Richard Widen finished it for his sister Florence's birthday and gave it to her in 1986, the year that Sean turned three. Richard Widen died that year, but his legacy lives on in his art and continues to inspire Sean and other young carvers. This sculpture is part of Sean's heritage, a heritage he carefully protects. "Nancy Clark gave me this piece by my dad," he says quietly. "It's the best sculpture of his I've ever seen. When I saw it, it just blew me away." The sculpture is part of Sean's past, but it is also part of his present and his future.

65: (facing) Two watchmen or *skil* flank Killer Whale, whose dorsal fin is as tall as their prestigious hats.

66: (left) *Bear Father* crest pole.

67: (above) Sean Brennan, whose Haida name is *Nunghlkayass.*

Recalling the distant past, he is well aware of how missionaries came to Haida Gwaii and cut down the crest poles, believing them to be objects of heathen worship—completely misunderstanding that they were public proclamations of clan rights and prerogatives expressed in a prestigious visual form. The crest poles were referred to as "totem poles", but this was incorrect—totemism was neither a crest pole's cultural concept nor its intent. Contrary to what some of the first foreign visitors to Haida Gwaii believed, these poles were not worshipped and held no religious connotations. The crests depicted on the poles are visual symbols of identity, family, lineage, and clan, reflecting unmistakeable ties to both Haida cultural prehistory and the lands this ancient nation occupies. As Sean carves the Bear and Raven pole, he thinks of great Haida artists from the 19th century such as Tom Price and John Robson. He knows their argillite masterpieces that are now recorded in books and kept in museums. He feels a connection to them.

Thinking about the present, Sean sees how Haida Gwaii is filled with the cycle of life and death. He understands that from this immutable cycle, memory deepens as heritage grows. "Being in the presence of great people" and hearing their potlatch speeches inspire him. The oratory has a broad range that on the one hand may celebrate life achievements or on the other bring together the grief-stricken and, through sharing, soften the edges of sorrow. As the argillite pole shifts in his hands and the fine chisel pushes through the stone, Sean remembers a young relative who died in a recent house fire. He thinks of a pole that will be carved in wood, a memorial pole; he thinks of who will carve it and the closure it will bring. His thoughts turn from that tragedy to the crest pole he is carving. It was partially inspired by the Bear Mother pole in Skidegate carved by Bill Reid, a 20th century master carver. Reid died in 1998, leaving behind a legacy both in artworks and in the Haida artists who owe a debt to his vision. Sean's pole is part heir to that legacy, but it was also inspired by a more contemporary event:

A week after Darren Swanson's potlatch when he became Chief Dadens and took the name ginaawaan, I went to Slatechuck for some argillite. I'd been thinking of doing a pole for a long time. I thought about Bill's Skidegate pole and the Bear Mother. I thought about the watchmen on the top of poles and Raven. Then I thought about the Sea Grizzly Chief's headdress that Ernie Swanson did for his uncle for the potlatch and I thought about Killer Whale and his great fin. I knew I was going to carve this pole as a response to different people who have inspired me.

Looking to the future, Sean is driven by his knowledge of Haida culture and art that he has accumulated from elders, peers, books, films, and his own experience. He has studied the formal aspects of formline design with Robert Davidson, taken a First Nations course in archaeology, and been inspired by other artists such as Jaalen Edenshaw, Chris Russ, and Vernon White. Father to Camellia and Ryleigh Jade, Sean helps to preserve the environment and the culture so that his daughters may grow up in a Haida Gwaii where people, their language and their arts flourish. "I want to keep carving, be recognized for my art, and leave a footprint on the island through my art, my kids," he says.

Sean's Haida name is *Nunghlkayass*, "The One I Found". The name belonged to his paternal uncle and, in a rare exception to the matrilineal inheritance of names, was formally given to him by an aunt who wanted him to be in her clan, *ts'a.ahl'laanaas* or the Eagle clan. Sean received the name at Robert Davidson's 2003 potlatch in Masset. After his adoption, he had to learn the name's meaning by speaking to the elders. It is from the elders that he has learned so much:

I've been trying to learn the Haida language for a few years now — it's become a little harder now since funding for the Haida Language Project has slowed down a bit. I love to hang out with the elders. I visit Stephen Brown to learn Haida. He and my naanii are both Eagles — he calls her "my sister" in the Haida way, so he calls me "my big grandson." I also spent time learning from people like Russell Samuels and Adelia Adams until they passed a couple of years ago. I used to go hunting and gathering chanterelles with Russell. The elders are inspiring. They open up gates to new thoughts for me. When I can't speak to them, I read the old stories from Masset and Skidegate recorded in books like Haida Texts and Myths.

Art has always been part of Sean's life. He began drawing as a child. "I always knew I wanted to be an artist," he says. Though his father died when he was very young, Sean saw argillite sculptures and pendants that had been kept in the family. The book *Pipes That Won't Smoke; Coal That Won't Burn*, a gift to his mother from his sister, was the first inspiration to carve argillite. "It had been lying around the house forever, and one day I picked it up and the first thing I wanted to do was to carve a panel pipe."

He began visiting the trailer where Cooper Wilson (his father-in-law), Donnie Edenshaw and Freddie Wilson carved. It was the beginning of a new direction in his art:

I just started hanging with those guys, soaking it all in. Then one day Cooper said, "Well, why don't you start carving?" I picked up a piece and just began working. I haven't really stopped since. At first I tried making drawings of what I wanted the sculpture to look like; it didn't work. So I threw away the drawings and just started carving and it came out like it appeared in my head.

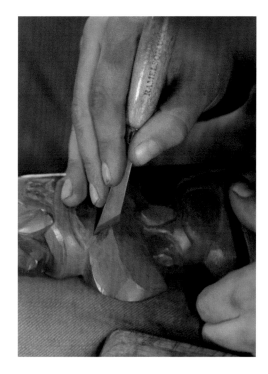

73

68: (facing) *Haida Shaman* by Sean Brennan's father Richard Widen. The Haida shaman wears a land otter headdress, symbolizing one of his supernatural helpers. He carries a round rattle and wears a bear claw necklace—all emblems of his profession as a healer.

69: (above) Sean uses a fine angled chisel to shape Raven's beak on the *Bear Father* crest pole.

Cooper was a good teacher. Some days he'd show me how to rough out a form, then other days he'd just be quiet and let me figure it out on my own. Sometimes he'd just show me the way to hold a chisel to get the right cut.

At first Sean tried carving pendants. Within a short time, he shifted his knowledge of traditional formline design from two dimensions to three. That was when he began seeing the world through different lenses. "I walk around forests all the time—it's my other job—and I get ideas about what I want to carve. I think in images," he says. But what he thinks and what argillite images evolve in his hands are not necessarily the same:

I like to look at a chunk of argillite and ask myself what could be in there. Most of the time, the image just pops out, but that doesn't apply to every piece. It's a piece-by-piece thing. It's all inside the stone more than it's in my head; it's more than me designing it. You don't just get an idea about what you want to carve and go find the right chunk of argillite. It's like those ancient Greek marble carvers. One of them said something like, "It's easy to be a sculptor because you just take away everything that's not supposed to be there."

To illustrate his point, Sean tells the story of a sculpture of three whales that he began to carve. Two of the whales came out fine, but the third one, he says, "just refused to be a whale, so I cut it off…and it became a shark." He glances up from carving, smiles.

Style is important to Sean, though he has a little trouble describing his own. He sees it as "still evolving," although one gallery owner described his work as "magical, spiritual, and imaginative—a new creation." Early on, Sean's work has taken on impressive dimensions. He quickly moved from carving simple pendants to the most challenging forms: the multiple figure tableaus on panel pipes and in canoes. Sean sometimes finds himself carving for hours without thinking about how the piece is taking shape. Sometimes he doesn't even know the character or where it's coming from:

I begin roughing out the stone and a story comes to me, the characters appear. When I work, I look for balance in the forms; they should have a nice flow and be organized. Balance is like the tide: there's an ebb and flow. There's a certainty in the movement, like the tide coming twice a day. Remember, we're a sea-going people.

Still, my art isn't too relaxed. I like to incorporate movement and expression. People say I put character in my carvings. I use a lot of piercings in the sculpture by removing negative space. Some forms are bunched up and are a kind of visual puzzle. Then comes the finishing. I spend a long time making the sculpture surfaces really nice. It's like taking the care to enter the longhouse in your best regalia—but it's also revealing your naked spirit.

74

70, 71: (facing) Right and left views of Sean's massive 45 cm *Journey of the Spirit Canoe*. Wasgo, Bear Mother and her cubs, Raven, Frog and a Shaman with his Octopus helper are on the journey.

Sean describes how inspiration and stone came together after he saw Bill Reid's *Spirit of Haida Gwaii—Jade Canoe* at the Vancouver International Airport. He had a piece of argillite at home in Old Masset, a big piece, long enough for a canoe. Nearly flawless, the stone spoke to his creative spirit. "I knew it wanted to be something like that," he says. He took six months to carve the canoe, beginning with a rough vessel shape, then ending with a powerful tableau of Haida supernatural creatures.

I didn't even know who was going to be in the canoe until I began carving it. Sarah would ask me, "Who is going to be in the canoe," and I would just say, "I don't know. They haven't shown up yet." Eventually all the characters jumped on the canoe as it was being carved. They all seemed to be on their way home. Home to Haida Gwaii.

The massive canoe remains one of Sean's favourite sculptures. Resting on its own base, the canoe is filled to capacity with supernatural creatures. Raven, *nang kilsdlaas*, was the first to emerge in the canoe as the forward paddler, befitting his legendary position as an essential figure in the pre-natal world of humankind. Sean depicts Raven as bird-like, but having human arms and hands that pull the paddle. The tip of Raven's paddle bears another of Sean's crests: Halibut. There is an urgency to

Raven; his beak is open, his wings blown back in the wind of this rapidly moving canoe.

The second figure to emerge was Octopus, the supernatural helper of shamans, but while that figure was still in the rough stages, Bear Mother and one of her cubs appeared. Like all mothers travelling with children, she appears a little anxious in the crowded transport. Her cub eagerly peers forward, trying to see past Raven's broad shoulders to where they are going.

The next figure to appear was the steersman: Wasgo or *suu sraa.n*, a supernatural sea-wolf. He is a mammoth sea monster who had the prowess and hunting skills of the wolf, but on a much larger scale. The principle prey of Wasgo was the killer whale; Sean's Wasgo has captured one in his large curly tail that he drags behind the canoe's stern.

When he'd finished carving the rest of the passengers, Sean returned to the complex figure of Octopus:

At first I thought I'd be carving a canoe with hunters in it who had been attacked by a giant octopus. I already knew from the form that the octopus was emerging from the waves and grabbing someone in the boat. It was clear to me from the beginning that there was going to be a human presence in the

72: (facing) Detail of *Journey of the Spirit Canoe* shows Raven, wings outspread, paddling. The blade of his paddle represents Halibut, a fish with both eyes on one side of its flat body. The paddle is inlaid with a mastodon ivory salmon-trout head in Halibut's body.

73: The supernatural sea monster Wasgo is the steersman in *Journey of the Spirit Canoe.* He has a head like a wolf, shown here with ivory teeth, a large dorsal fin, and a massive curling tail that is capable of carrying his favourite prey: killer whales. Note that this Wasgo has human hands that grip his paddle.

78

74: (above) In the bow of Sean's *Journey of the Spirit Canoe* is a shaman. His supernatural helper, Octopus, has nearly engulfed him. Frantically, he pulls back the tentacles from around his face so he can speak, though he remains blinded by the heavy coils of the devilfish. Peering from beneath the shaman is Frog.

75: (facing) Frog—one of Sean's personal crests.

canoe. But as the carving progressed, I realized that there was a mythological struggle happening here, a spiritual event.

This wasn't a hunter, but a shaman in the bow of the canoe and I was carving Octopus, his spiritual helper, trying to "speak through" the human. I asked myself how I could breathe it through the stone. There was this over-whelming sense of Octopus speaking, yet the shaman was totally smothered. You can see that the tentacles are wrapped around the shaman's head; his eyes are covered. He has one big hand pulling the tentacle away from his mouth, freeing himself to speak. It was the way the argillite wanted me to carve it.

The canoe's last occupant was Frog. He crouches under the writhing tentacles, in front of Raven. He gazes wide-eyed at the viewer, unmoved by the tumultuous struggle above his head. Frog is one of Sean's crests; here on the canoe, it is a symbol of his participation in the journey.

For Sean Brennan, the journey is paramount. He strives to carve full-time, developing more motivation and commitment to his art with every argillite sculpture that leaves his hands. "There is more to carving than just the tools and the slate," he says. "There's a lot of time and thinking that goes into each piece, a lot of me." He's confident about the future of argillite art and its continuity with the past 200 years of this art's history:

I feel an amazing sense of pride in being Haida. Everything is growing in Haida Gwaii: we're growing as a people, as a whole nation. Some other cultures don't know their heritage or have been oppressed for a long time. I'm happy about how strong our nation is because it's been strong for a long time. There's a definite security here — lots of opportunity. I feel that for my children. I want that for them. They'll know who they are and they'll know their history. Other people outside of Haida Gwaii will know it too. My argillite art contributes to that as argillite has always done. When argillite leaves Haida Gwaii, it's like sending postcards to the universe: "Hey! This is Haida!"

Sean Brennan's art almost always travels off-island, sometimes to faraway places. His sculptures embody uniquely Haida perspectives, yet their appeal rests in bringing forth shared human experience. Through bold and thought-provoking images in argillite, Sean sends an invitation for understanding a people, a culture, and a spirit as he petitions for an appreciation of all it means to be "going home to Haida Gwaii".

79

MICHAEL JOHN BROWN
Qunce-sgan

By conventional North American standards, Mike Brown lives humbly in a small one-room cabin overlooking Skidegate Inlet. By Haida standards, he lives richly, close to the land, intimate with the spirits of Haida Gwaii. It's a choice, he explains, to live an uncomplicated life, in communion with the land, the people and the culture. By his standards, he lives well. There's no running water inside the cabin. His workbench, covered in tools and black argillite dust, is in front of a window overlooking the tidal flats and his small garden. In a corner chair, a yellow cat lounges beneath a tiny rubber ball hanging from the ceiling. The ball, a miniature blue earth, is intended for feline amusement. One wonders if it is also a sardonic comment by this environmentally conscious man. Incongruously, next to the cat's chair rests an expensive set of golf clubs, glowing dully in the corner. ("Yeah," Mike says ironically, "I got 'em in a thrift store! I used to golf with some buddies who needed a designated driver.")

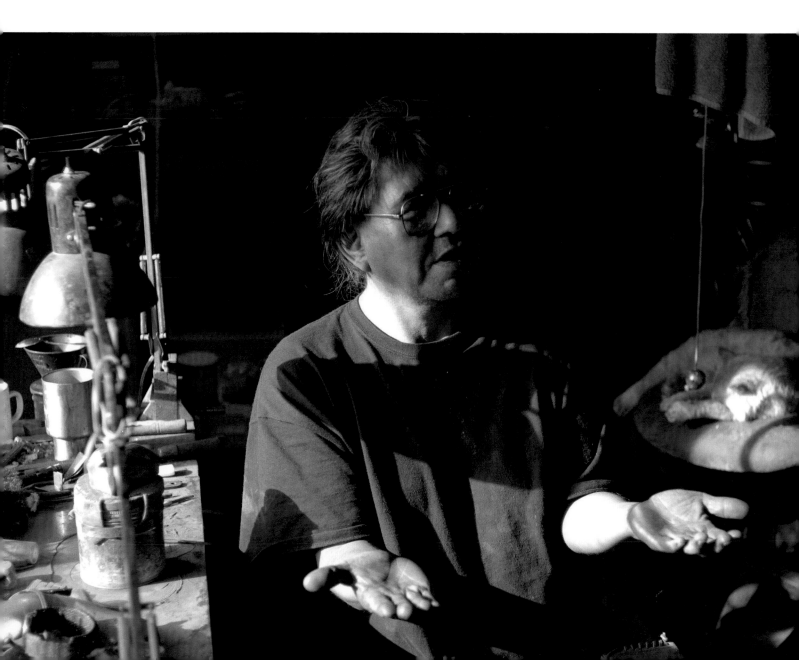

Books are piled everywhere. An elbow lamp illuminates the argillite beneath Mike's chisel. He peers at it through large thick lenses, pushes the blade along the stone, blows away the dust. Behind him, a large flat-screen TV, its sound muted, fills the back of the cabin, crowding a bed. Everything is covered with fine gray dust, even Mike. His gentle smile and sharp wit reveal a man not only content but also engaged with life. It's a short walk to the beach to collect firewood, crabs or oysters; it's a little longer walk into town to gather supplies, do laundry, collect the mail, and meet with the people who will buy his argillite art. It's a good life.

His story, Mike explains, begins with his heritage. He's proud to be the grandson of Percy Andrew Brown (d. 1979) and the great-grandson of Captain Andrew Brown (1879-1962), who was a well-known and prolific carver of argillite poles and canoes. Originally from the village of Yan and later from Old Masset, Captain Brown's Haida name was *Owt'iwans* or "Big Eagle". Mike remembers that at age six he met Captain Brown:

He was a kinda cranky old man by the time he came from Hydaburg—that's my Alaskan heritage—to Yan, where he met his wife Susan. Then they moved to Old Masset. He was an amazing, skilled man: a carpenter, a mechanic, a fisherman, and a boat builder. He worked along with Claude Davidson and his dad, building a lot of the seine fleet. He built the Ruth G. (1 and 2), *the* Haida Warrior, *and the* Monarch. *That's how he got the name Captain Brown.*

I remember that he was always carving. After his wife died, he just lost the will to live and he died a few years later. I didn't know him that well. I heard about how when he got bored he'd carve the handles of his tools and cover them with figures of Bear and Eagle and other crests. Those tools went to Archie Abraham's house and then were lost in a house fire. My grandfather Percy was real sad when that happened.

He remarks that a great many of his great-grandfather's poles are in museums and can still be found in galleries and in on-line auctions, selling for handsome prices. Indeed, Captain Brown is frequently mentioned in scholarly works as a prolific argillite artist, but he is also referred to as a consultant to some of the leading ethnographers who visited Haida Gwaii. Of his great-grandfather's work as an artist, Mike says proudly:

His work is found all over the world. He was a great traveller, going up and down the coast from Alaska to California selling his poles. He went to California because he heard the ancestors went there to get abalone and he wanted to see for himself. He brought back some big abalone shells. He also travelled to Brazil. I know about this because he brought back shell beads from there and my family still had those beads after he died.

81

76: (facing) Michael's modest studio home. This argillite artist has been carving for over 30 years.

77: (above) Michael Brown.

Mike recalls that as a youngster he heard his elders speaking Haida all around him. He understood the language and spoke it a little, though now he says the language is harder to hear and harder to speak. "Sometimes, I think people are ashamed to speak it. I'm grateful for the work on our language done by John Enrico and Margaret Blackman. Now the real hope for the language is in the children who are learning Haida in school."

Mike's grandfather Percy was a fisherman, who ran Captain Brown's boats. Percy was also a carver despite losing two fingers in a fishing accident. Fluent in the Haida language and culture, he believed in a traditional way of life and raising children. When Mike was eight, his mother, Pauly Naomi, was willing to send him away to Mormon school, but his grandfather intervened:

The day they came to get me, Grandfather stopped them. He just threw them off the porch. It was the first time I saw a Mormon fly. Then my Grandfather turned to me and told me to go play. I'll never forget that; I was one of the lucky ones.

Four years later, my mother drowned. I remember her as a talented woman. She was good with her hands: good at sewing blouses and making bread. She was the hairdresser for the village, doing lots of perms for the ladies. Most of the members of my family ran stores or businesses of some kind. Some of them still do.

His *naanii* Ruth and *tsinii* Percy raised him after his mother died. Mike also had the benefit of knowing many of his uncles and relatives from the Alaskan side of the family, who contributed to his traditional education. Belonging to the K'owaas Eagle clan, Mike received the Haida name *Qunce-sgan*, "King Killer Whale", from his grandfather. "I'm the last of that family, though I still have some aunties and uncles from the other side." After attending Tahayghen Elementary School in Old Masset, he went to George M. Dawson High School and "finished grade 11-and-a-half."

When he was 16, Mike began carving argillite with Donald Edgars and members of the Yeltatzie family: Terry, Harold, Richard, John, and George. Every day after his job washing floors in the cannery, he'd join them around a table where he learned about tools, design and technique. In his 20s he carved wood and worked with Christian White building traditional Haida canoes. "I learned to do it all: wood, silver, argillite — but it was always argillite that I wanted to do."

At first he concentrated on making argillite pendants, but quickly moved on to fully dimensional sculptures and plates when he realized people wouldn't pay him what he figured his pendants were worth. "I just wouldn't drop my prices." In Vancouver, he remembers the successful sale of his first Bear Mother sculpture:

I took it to the gallery and they wanted it really bad, but they just couldn't afford it. There was a couple there who overheard what I was asking. When I left the shop, they ran after me and said they'd pay my price. Just like that. I was real happy. Things like that have happened to me a lot.

Like his great-grandfather before him, Mike had many occupations: dishwasher, ditch digger, tree planter and, for two weeks, a logger. For four and one-half years he worked on the Parks Canada boat delivering mail supplies to the Haida Watchmen in Gwaii Haanas National Park. The Watchmen's duties are to protect the ecologically and culturally sensitive sites and to educate visitors about the cultural values and traditions of the ancestors who lived in villages such as *Kuuna* (Skedans), *T'aanuu* (Tanu), and *Skun Gwaii* (Ninstints). It was a job that suited him well:

I worked for the government — 28 dollars an hour — low man on the totem pole. We worked banker's hours from 8 to 5, ten days on and four days off, which wasn't so bad. And of course it was during the summer, so we had all

78: From his workbench, Michael uses a variety of tools to finish the *Raven Discovering the First People in a Clamshell* sculpture. He has carved it in two pieces: the Raven in flight and the clamshell base. Later he joined them together seamlessly.

late afternoon and evening to ourselves. The work was interesting, I was fed every day, had a warm dry place to sleep every night, daily showers, and TV; it was almost better than being at home! All that sunshine from 5 to about 11 at night. I used to carve every day, sometimes until late at night. It was fun. I'm one of the few Haidas who have seen all of Haida Gwaii. From Cape St. James to North Island to Rose Spit. It's all my grandfather told me. The animals out there, beyond where most people go, are just fabulous.

But eventually, he says, "I got tired of working at regular jobs. All I wanted to do was carve. I worked 19 years, paid all my taxes, quit working, and became my own boss. Carving took over my life." Mike has been carving for over 30 years.

Inspired by the old versions of Haida traditional stories that he heard from Percy, Mike strives to create new images from the narratives. One of his favourite stories is Raven coaxing humans out of their primordial clamshell. It's a theme that he's frequently commissioned to do, though each time he interprets it the image is completely new and fresh.

Mike tries to imagine the conversations that surround the images, the sounds and expressions that the characters make. In one sculpture depicting Raven, the Creator bird seems startled into flight as the humans begin to emerge from the clamshell. One human backs out, slinging his arm over the top shell. He's clutching an elbow adze: the first carver in Haida Gwaii. Surprised, Raven opens his mouth in an irate protest. Sometimes the stone itself brings its own surprises:

Surprises? All the time! Always—it never turns out the way you want it. You're doing the work for it, not the other way around. You're just there to chip away at the stone so whatever's in there can come out. Sometimes the shape is already in the rock.

I just begin by looking at the argillite. Sometimes it's the chunk that tells you what it wants to be. Like this one piece. I could see a figure coming out one side of the stone—a bear's head. I only had to cut out the other side of the piece. Sometimes I can feel what's in there, inside the stone. I just have to work on the shape—then I reach a point when I say, "Oh! That's what it wants to be. Cool." And I keep going until it's finished.

79: (left) In R*aven Discovering the First People in a Clamshell,* Michael's Raven seems spooked into flight by what he's found on the beach—a shell full of men. Note the bird face in the tail between Raven's outstretched wings.

80: (below) From the left side of the clam shell, the first carpenter is backing out, rear end first, carrying an elbow-adze, a tool used for roughing out large wooden objects: everything from crest poles to feast dishes. His arm, draped over the top of the shell, has startled Raven into flight.

86

True to the Haida convention of carving argillite pipes concealed beneath complicated tableaus of intertwined and interactive natural and supernatural creatures, Mike's panel pipes first challenge the viewer to discern pipe bowl and stem. All the pipes are drilled through the stem to the bowl, and theoretically, though not practically, they could be smoked. (It might be an expensive puff, since argillite is prone to crack or shatter from heat.) When he lived in Victoria, Mike often visited the Royal British Columbia Museum and Archives, looking at argillite and the tools that earlier generations of Haida used to carve it:

Some of the panel pipes were 18 inches long and less than a half inch thick. I'd ask myself, "How did they do that?" That helped me design a special tool for my own pipes. I still drill the holes in the pipe first and then carve the images around it. It's safer that way, given my wonky eyes.

One of his sculptures depicts four frogs, a pair facing each end, that adorn the top of a pipe supported by a long pipe stem. The pipe bowl is concealed in the body of the end frog. At the stem end of the pipe a frog's tongue protrudes to the tip. At the bowl end, two frogs exchange tongues, or as Mike describes it, "they're exchanging stories." Frogs were important crests among the Haida and figure prominently in Haida mythology. In some stories, grizzly bears are mortally afraid of frogs; in others, the amphibians are so terrified of bears that they hold a conference and decide to abandon Haida Gwaii.

Mike trusts in the longevity of his argillite sculpture to represent him in a world he deems decidedly small and struggling. Heritage is important to him. "And I'm happy to hand it down," he says. Occasionally a nephew or some other visitor will drop by for a carving lesson and he's happy to accommodate because he believes in the future of this art and his responsibility to help advance it. In his small cabin he will lend them his tools and share his experience in carving. "I'll help anyone," he says:

It took a long time for people to knock on my door, but now some of them want to come and learn. I show them some of my tools and explain that they don't have to be expensive to be effective. Some tools only cost $6 to $10. "Why waste that money on booze," I say to them. Sometimes they don't have the money for the gas to get their boat to Slatechuck, so I'll just give them a chunk of argillite. Then sometimes they'll come back and bring me a fish by way of gratitude.

I tell them that carving's a hard profession to get into, but don't give up; keep trying. When I give talks in the schools, I always urge students to finish their education before they try to get into the art business. It's important to have a good education.

Though he misses every piece of his sculpture that leaves his hands, Mike finds some consolation in the photographs he keeps of his work.

81: (upper facing) *Frog Pipe.* The sharing of tongues on this panel pipe represents "exchanging stories," according to Michael. Frog is an important Eagle crest among the Haida, frequently appearing on poles and dance masks. Frogs are also characters in stories from supernatural times.

82: (lower facing) Inspired by early 19th century panel pipes Michael has seen in museum collections, his *Haida Stories Panel Pipe* portrays a frog, salmon, two killer whales, a bear with two bear cubs, a human and a raven, all major figures in stories of Haida Gwaii.

Photos are neatly filed, away from the ubiquitous argillite dust, in several albums. He also finds a certain pride in all it means to be Haida, though, ever the vigilant ecologist, he says with some irony:

While I'm glad to be one of the guys keeping argillite art alive, I'd feel prouder if I'd been born a thousand years ago. It's sad to see the islands dwindling, to see the people dwindling too. And they're still taking the trees out of here.

I could be rich like some famous Haida carvers, but I don't want to be. Money may help with some things, but it's not everything. It's been a good road, carving.

Finding satisfaction in knowing his work has reached collections far beyond his small footprint in Haida Gwaii, Mike Brown celebrates the idea that argillite sculpture almost always travels far from its place of origin. "Argillite art brings the Haida recognition. It says, '*Hey world — we're here!*'"

83: (facing) *Chief Bearing Gifts* panel pipe. Four canoe men transport a Haida chief to an important event. The chief, who wears a frontlet headdress and is holding a Raven staff, brings gifts in two bentwood boxes between the forward rower and second paddler. The pipe bowl is contained in the bentwood box's lid. The steersman holds a bear rattle; his paddle has an eagle formline design on it. The stem of the pipe, fully drilled to connect with the bowl, is below the canoe stern.

84: (above) Environmentally conscientious, this artist lives in a modest cabin with a priceless view of Skidegate Inlet, looking from his Graham Island home south to Moresby Island.

GRYN WHITE
Duugwi.is

Siorra, dark eyes wide, skips across the living room and hooks a tiny arm around her father's knee. Her Celtic name means "Warrior Princess" and she does indeed have all the qualities of royalty. Her father, Gryn White, has a Haida name, *Duugwi.is*, meaning "Strong Haida", and he too is descended from an impressive lineage of Haida artists that has attained almost royal status in the art world. It is to this legacy that Gryn feels a deep sense of duty and responsibility; it is part of the force that drives him to persevere in creating art.

Gryn's great great grandfather was Charles Edenshaw (1839–1920), *Tahayghen* (also written *da.a xiiang*), a chief of the *StA'stas* Eagle clan whose fame has stretched from the 19th to the 21st centuries. Many people consider him the most influential Haida artist, though there is also agreement that for a time his reputation may have overshadowed many other comparably impressive figures. Scholars are still unravelling the broader picture of Haida artistic achievement as a more complete art history is reconstructed. Still, Edenshaw's legacy, through his work in argillite, wood, ivory, gold and silver, reflects undeniable strength, vitality, and excellence that has passed through the generations.

One of Charles Edenshaw's granddaughters is Lavina White (*T'how-hegelths* or "The Sound of Many Copper Shields"), the daughter of Emily Edenshaw and Henry White. She is a woman always ahead of her time, who carved argillite and made silkscreen prints as early as 1962, when few aboriginal women were recognized as artists. A distinguished social, environmental and political activist, she was President of the Council of the Haida Nation in 1977, one of the first women in Canada to hold such a leadership position. Her sons, Henry White, Greg Lightbown, Bill Lightbown, Jr., and Shane Lightbown, followed in her footsteps to become exceptional artists. Their argillite sculpture has found its way into international private and public collections.

Greg Lightbown, an argillite carver for over 40 years, is Gryn's father; Gryn's mother is Lynn Cherry. (The name Gryn is a combination of his parent's names.) Because he was born on a full moon, his mother named him *Konai,* the Haida word for "moon". It was his naanii Lavina, however, who decided he "wasn't a 'Gryn'" and gave him the name *Duugwi.is.* From the Raven clan, his crests are Bear, Killer Whale, and Shark. He credits his grandmother with "pushing him along" to become an artist when his parents at first tried to discourage him because of the profession's unpredictability and the certainty of life struggles if he were to follow in his elders' footsteps.

Gryn chose art. He began carving argillite in his early teens, helping to rough out pendants for his father. After high school, he moved from Old Masset to Vancouver, where he attended Langara Community College and took fine arts courses in design and art history:

85: (facing) Gryn White with his family: Tara and their daughter Siorra.

86: (left) This small argillite crest pole depicts Dogfish Woman at the top with Grizzly Bear at the bottom. The dogfish's uneven-lobed tail rises above her pointed fin to dramatically top the pole.

87: (below) Gryn has carved the dogfish to show many of her identifying characteristics: a large domed forehead with three gill slits and sharp interlocking teeth. She has a large disk-shaped lip plug or labret, indicating her high rank and wealth, as well as a beak-like nose that curves into the mouth: a symbol of her transformative powers.

At Langara, I gained an appreciation of all types of art, especially modern art, but I learned how to appreciate art in general, to be more observant. I studied how art reflects the culture it comes from and the differences and similarities between art forms in other cultures. This appreciation gave me another way to approach what I knew about Haida art, to see the refined rules of design and how precise our art is.

I learned human and animal forms from life drawing classes, how to design spaces, and the importance of perspective and balance in design. It was a little like studying math to unravel different art methods. It gave me the chance to train my eye to see — to take the time to observe and perfect my ability to translate my vision to my own art.

Gryn was particularly impressed with learning about contemporary art, what he describes as its "raw aspects" of seeing and identifying negative space, balance, symmetry, shape, line and form. He was then able to take that awareness back to what he knew of Haida design principles and apply it to the "rules" of formline design:

There's something about the beautiful shapes of ovoids, U forms and split-U forms. There is a balance and flow to them just as there is to the formline, which swells really wide, then narrows to almost nothing when it approaches another formline. It's awesome.

I began to see the rules of Haida design as deeply rooted in our culture. It gave me the understanding of what Charles Edenshaw and Tom Price had achieved, and what Bill Reid restored to Haida art. They became my teachers.

I'm still learning the rules and how I can perfect them within my own style. I like trying to stick to these rules, not deviate or tamper with them, but explore them. There's so much to learn from the old style designs. I want to create contemporary Haida art within these traditional boundaries. I'm not much interested in coming up with a new form of Haida art. I want to honour and feel continuity with the past.

For this season in his life, Gryn is more than content to work at creating Haida art that falls within traditional design conventions because he doesn't find the process particularly confining. While he speculates that he may one day attempt another art form outside Haida art, he sees that day in the distant future. For now, he's immersed in a spirit of learning about the traditional forms, finding the parameters of experimenting with them, and exploring the tension between being confined to "old style" rules and original innovation. He's clear that he wants to honour and show appreciation for the past in his work, yet develop his own perspective and style:

I want to take inspiration from the old masters' work, yet also feel free to do something interesting that pops into my head based on my knowledge of Haida stories and art forms. My art's evolving, but I want to contribute to the conti-

nuity of Haida art, not dilute its power. I'd like my work to be seen as staying true to its origins. There is always tension in art — and the pitfalls of trying different paths. But rather than put the brakes on my creative efforts, I just want to focus on the task at hand, play on the tension in art that is between the design form and being creative.

Gryn has been particularly inspired by Charles Edenshaw, whose work he describes as "the ultimate, the absolute perfection of Haida art." He has studied Edenshaw's plates and argillite boxes in books and in museum collections. Seeing the pieces first-hand has given him the inspiration to study traditional Haida stories and to see how creatively Edenshaw brought them to life in his sculptures. Gryn especially appreciates his ancestor's artistic and intellectual skills:

He was perfect, brilliant — one of the greatest artists in the world. He's known for the beauty of his work and the amount of thought he put into every image. It's awesome to think of the impact he's had for Northwest Coast art! Understanding him is to understand the heritage behind all that he did; his biography helps us comprehend Haida thought.

He proudly acknowledges his father as his strongest inspiration. Greg Lightbown, a member of what the popular press has dubbed "the family that carves," was one of four sons who took up argillite carving under Lavina's influence. From the time he was a small boy, Gryn recognized that he wanted to be like his father:

93

It was wonderful growing up with him. Art came to me almost as second nature because, when I was young, he was always drawing and carving. He's something of an entrepreneur; he always has something creative on the go.

88: Gryn's work station holds an unfinished Raven sculpture beneath a sketch for a large argillite panel. Some argillite sculptors work directly from what they see in the stone; others, like Gryn, find an idea in the argillite, then perfect the sculpture's image on paper before they carve it.

Of course there was the negative side too: sometimes he was so involved with carving that he didn't have much time for me.

On the positive side, his work, like the panel pipe with the transformation hawk/man and the killer whale, and that sculpture of the supernatural dancer transforming into a bird illustrated in the Glenbow book, just inspired me over and over again. In a way, they make me a little envious of him. I've never said that to him, it's just one of those unspoken things, but my dad's still better than I am, and I'm still trying to get to his level. I'd like to think I'm well on my way, though.

Gryn continues to move forward in his own development as an argillite sculptor. An avowed perfectionist, he continues to refine his process. He finds himself contemplating Haida stories that he has read or heard first-hand from the elders. The stories become the substance of daydreams, then the images find their way on to paper. Like his father, he first works on ideas in two-dimensional formline design, then translates them to three-dimensional forms. He's filled many sketchbooks with his ideas, working out proportions, balance, and stylistic problems. Some of the designs never make it to the argillite; other times, the stone's shape suggests a form. "I'll go with the shape of the rock, get an idea, then draw it, then I go back to the rock. It tells me more. I may see a head, a fin, a face coming out of the body of the argillite."

He describes feeling connected to the stone; the chunk of argillite usually influences how he approaches the piece and what images he incorporates in sculpting it. Gryn feels that his style is ever changing, evolving. "I'm still exploring, still learning." he says. He's found he can innovate within the traditional boundaries, putting silver bear heads on the sides of an argillite box, for example, or incorporating a fine twist of catlinite around a Bear Mother tableau on a box lid.

His sculptures contain subtle surprises. A sculpture of Killer Whale is deceptively accessible. At first glance it looks like a killer whale should, with its large dorsal fin, massive toothed jaws, and a bifurcated tail tucked under its body. On closer examination, however, Killer Whale's fierce expression draws the viewer closer. Gryn has inlaid the open mouth with an arched catlinite tongue. The idea of ferocity changes to one of rage; this animal is shrieking. Why? Gryn has placed a human face in the orca's dorsal fin. The storyline becomes clearer: this is Gunarh, the husband of the woman this supernatural being has kidnapped. The man tenaciously grips the sides of the animal, determined to ride to the depths of the ocean to rescue his wife from the undersea village of the Killer Whale People.

Gryn's style is one of meticulous blends of two and three-dimensional design. His use of inlay is precise, balanced. He uses abalone inlay to draw our eyes to the subtleties of the forms, and catlinite inlay

89: (upper facing) Gryn's *Bear Mother* box combines complex two-dimensional formline design on the sides of the box with sculptural heads that emerge from each panel. The sides of the box have large bear heads, while the box's front panel shows a transformation face with a beak-like nose that re-curves into the mouth. Frogs support each corner of the box.

90: (lower facing) Inside a ring of catlinite on the lid of this impressive box, Gryn has carved a Bear Mother and her supernatural Bear husband. Filled with evocative images, this traditional Haida story tells of a high-ranking woman who is seduced by a man in the woods. He convinces her to marry him; then, after returning to his village, discovers she has married a supernatural Bear and will give birth to his half-human, half-Bear children. Gryn has often explored this theme of the ultimate cross-cultural marriage in his sculptures.

91: (right) *Gunarh and the Killer Whale.* The intensity of this supernatural killer whale's movement is unmistakable. Enraged, it vaults above the water. This is one of the Killer Whale People, *sqaana xaaydagaay*, with its large dorsal fin, a round blowhole over the forehead, and a bifurcated tail that curls back toward its body.

92: (lower left) Gryn has carved an arched catlinite tongue inside the orca's mouth, giving it a convincing appearance of rage.

92: (lower right) In Killer Whale's dorsal fin, the artist has portrayed a human face in low relief. The shoulders, arm, forearm and hand of the hero, Gunarh, are merely incised into the orca's skin. The man, determined to recover his kidnapped wife, clings to the whale so tightly that his form has merged with that of the mammal.

96

to emphasize power and tension in supernatural encounters. It is a mistake to take this artist for granted; there are always hidden meanings, moments of transformation, and wonderful visual puns to uncover in a Gryn White sculpture.

He's also evolving in his approach to the business of art, completing a course in business administration and developing a business plan to further his own marketing potential. Gryn is aware of the need to grow laterally as he develops new skill sets such as printmaking and casting argillite into signed and numbered limited-edition pieces in silver. He sees himself looking for more business opportunities, meeting more people, and building stronger relationships with collectors and galleries. He can envision the day when he has his own gallery and helps other artists.

For the moment, though, his passion remains creating argillite sculpture. While he'll occasionally design and engrave silver for his wife Tara (*Tl'aaguula*) and Siorra, he makes a living carving argillite. When the pieces leave his hands, he has mixed feelings of loss on the one hand and pride in promoting Haida culture on the other:

Sometimes when the pieces go, I feel a little lost. Ideally, I'd like to keep everything I make—you just get attached to them when you spend so long on each one. I put everything I have into these sculptures: a piece of myself, my spirit. The up side is knowing that I can give that to someone, the collector. That rejuvenates my energy for doing the next piece. There's no getting over the sense of loss when a sculpture leaves my hands. You don't get over it; you get used to it.

When I send an argillite sculpture out into the world, it's a partial fulfilment of my duty to carry on the legacy for my family, for my dad and my great great grandfather. I'm a link in the chain and I believe in doing my part to take care of this lineage, to contribute to Haida culture, so I can pass it down to my daughter. The whole art form—especially argillite sculpture—is so ingrained in the culture that it enables us to move forward, to ensure the longevity of Haida Gwaii and its people—for eternity.

I'm proud to be Haida, proud of my culture. Lots of people in the world don't have an idea about their own culture. My culture is part of my home, my roots, part of who I am and how I define myself. When I create these works, they connect me to Haida Gwaii; when people connect with my art, it also brings them to some understanding of being Haida, of living here. I want to be perceived as contributing to the continuity of Haida life.

Identity and meaning, tradition and legacy are combined in Gryn White's sculpture. His art connects him to Haida Gwaii, to respect and appreciation for the people, land and animals of his island home. He values the richness of Haida history and culture; through his artwork, he conveys those values to a world hungry for meaning.

SHAUN EDGARS
Luguud

94: (above) Shaun Edgars works on a salmon sculpture in his kitchen.

95: (upper facing) Luguud or "Waving Shield" is also an accomplished singer and drummer.

96: (lower facing) After inlaying the abalone eyes of the Salmon People within the salmon image, Shaun begins fine tool-finishing the sculpture.

Disarming, eager to share, Shaun Edgars motions his visitor to a chair in his kitchen and brings tea to the table. Beyond his window seat, the tide is changing in Masset Inlet; above, pearly grey skies swirl as the wind whips the rushing water into frothy waves. Eagles and ravens tumble in the sky, then swoop down to the emerging beach. The retreating tide has left their lunch among the rocks.

Like the images he carves in argillite, Shaun conveys warmth and accessibility. As he speaks, his hands are busy working on a sculpture of a great salmon. Occasionally, he glances at the ever-changing landscape outside the kitchen window, pausing, chisel suspended above the stone, as he reads the currents in sky and water. For a moment, it's as if he too were flying with the ravens, cavorting with eagles. Then he's back, smiling, engaged. Shaun speaks excitedly about his own personal history, his gaze riveted on his work as he smoothes the knife marks on the salmon's gills. His focus is intense as he examines each pass of the tool, repeatedly blowing the dust away from its blade. The abalone-inlaid eye of the massive fish gleams, almost surrealistically animating the head.

The salmon Shaun is carving is slightly smaller than life size, but in terms of its presence, both artistically and spiritually, it's monumental. This is no ordinary salmon, it is a supernatural being symbolized by the three human faces emerging from the fish's body, hands gripping its fins and gills. Seen as if the fish's body were transparent, the faces are those of the Salmon People. Glimpsed as human spirits, they are seen returning in the salmon to their natal stream. Surrounded by salmon eggs, they bring the gift of life to the Haida people, and in return the Haida honour the salmons' homecoming to the creeks and rivers, welcoming them with song and prayers.

Each year when the salmon run begins, the people of Haida Gwaii gather for a special ceremony. The first salmon is caught and eaten and the bones are carefully burned or returned to the water. They do this in the belief that the supernatural salmon will regenerate and return to the village of the Salmon People below the ocean. There, the animals shed their fish disguises to resume a human appearance. Deep beneath the surface they live in human-style longhouses in a world that looks much like the Northwest Coast. The following year, the journey from the sea to Haida Gwaii is repeated, and the Haida gratefully accept the food of their offered bodies, respecting and honouring the Salmon People's gift. Shaun's sculpture *Return of the Sockeye* is another expression of the theme of death and reincarnation, but is also a meaningful lesson in cultural ecology.

Shaun has commemorated this journey of the Salmon People in argillite and in song, based on his first-hand knowledge of Haida culture and environments. His naanii, Violet Edgars, was instrumental in raising and training him in traditional food gathering and hunting techniques as well as sharing foundational Haida cultural knowledge. When he shot his first deer, she instructed him in the hunt, to respect his prey and how to use all parts of the animal. With her instruction he's learned to love gathering food—clam digging, fishing, picking seaweed, and catching devilfish. It's taken a few years, but Shaun now credits her and his tsinii Frank Edgars for giving him "a sense of awe for what our grandfathers perfected."

I appreciate the toughness of the old tsiniis. Like my tsinii Frank Edgars. He used to go deer hunting even when he was on crutches. He didn't complain. He just did what he had to do to get food in. I admire all the old people and what they did to keep themselves and this culture alive.

The things that make being Haida important to me are just going out and practising all aspects of our culture that our tsiniis and naaniis and their tsiniis and naaniis did as a way of life. When I say all aspects, I mean not just the art forms, but story telling, language, dancing, food gathering, medicine gathering. Not just learning it, but applying it every day and teaching our children at an early age.

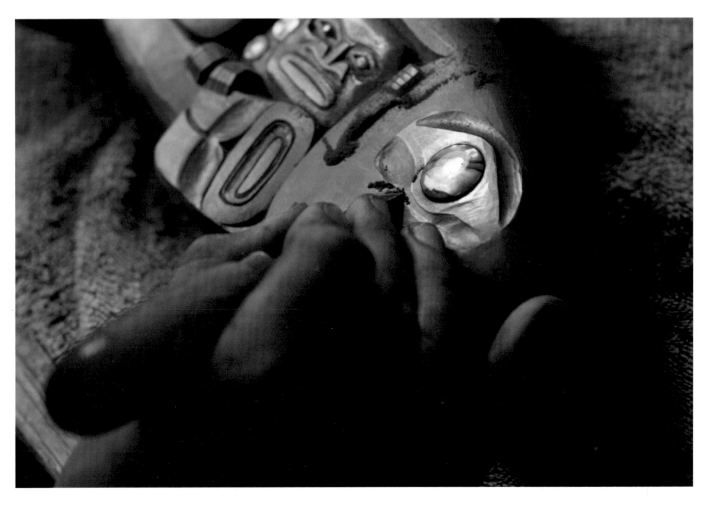

Shaun received the name *Luguud* or "Waving Shield" from his naanii
Mary Swanson. From the *Yaɬh'laanaas* Raven clan, originally from the
village of Dadens (*daa.adans*) on Langara Island, Shaun comes from
a long line of artists. His great great grandmother was Emily White
(1880-1972), a daughter of the famous Haida artist Charles Edenshaw.
His Haida parents are both artists. His mother, Tina Edgars, sews fine
button blankets, while his father, Monty Stewart Burton, carves wood
and engraves gold and silver. They, along with artists such as Cooper
Wilson, Jim Hart, Christian White, and especially Donnie Edenshaw,
have influenced him in the pursuit of a career in argillite carving:

*I began hanging around Donnie, watching him carve. One day he just said,
"Gees, why don't you just pick up some tools and get carving?" I first did a little
Raven pendant in 1993. Donnie kind of took me under his wing and showed
me some techniques. Soon all I wanted to do was carve argillite. I started
making some small sculptures of little bears, but I was totally fascinated by the
carving of this huge eagle that he was doing. I looked at my little bears and it
didn't take long for me to figure out that I was putting in a lot of time on these
small things when I could be doing something big like Donnie. So I ran up the
mountain and got myself a big chunk. That's when I started doing larger pieces.*

Large or small, Shaun's argillite sculptures are dynamic, often showing the figure as if it were animated — transforming from the natural world into the art world. Shaun's argillite animals are not static, they are in motion, perhaps because he sees them as having natural forms with the potential to become supernatural creatures. For example, an argillite pendant in the form of the great Halibut shows the animal swimming, head up, tail pressing down. When Shaun creates large sculptures he also depicts the subject moving through space, informed by what he sees in nature and what he imagines in the spirit world.

Shaun brings to his art what he's observed through his own life experiences. His principle occupation for the last 17 years has been as a commercial fisherman, a job he's not fond of because he's prone to seasickness. Going below the waves, however, is another story. As a certified scuba diver, Shaun spent four years making research dives for marine biologists studying sea urchin and abalone populations. During that time he had many opportunities to visit all the ancient maritime villages of Gwaii Haanas:

For the last few years with my job diving, I've been lucky to go to the old villages around Haida Gwaii. I've been able to study lots of old poles in their

97: Shaun's supernatural salmon carries three humans whose faces are seen within the fish's body as if it were transparent. They are the Salmon People, returning to their natal stream with the gift of life for the Haida. Circles of abalone inset into the salmon's body represent the salmon eggs that the homecoming fish will lay before dying. The spirit of the salmon is thus reborn – the salmon fry will leave their birthplace to live in their underwater villages before swimming again to their freshwater origins. Their cyclical journey of life and death mirrors the traditional Haida belief in reincarnation and regeneration.

98: (above) The *tc a'maos* (meaning "tide-walker) or Sea Grizzly was a creature of both sea and land. Resembling a bear with a large dorsal fin, it is a Raven crest belonging primarily to clans from Skidegate, Ninstints and Rose Spit.

99: (facing) Shaun's *Sea Grizzly* has typical bear features: a large square snout with great curling nostrils, sharp pointed teeth, large claws on its paws, and ears over the forehead. Behind the bear's massive arms are pectoral fins, attesting to its ability to swim in the ocean as easily as it walks on land.

natural state. It meant a lot to me to be able to be where old Haida values and traditions were obviously practised and to appreciate how closely the ancestors were connected to the land and sea. In the ancient villages I saw first hand what wisdom, strength and respect the Haida had for their homeland and what we must have for it now.

In his travels above and below the seas, Shaun has encountered almost every variety of marine life in Haida Gwaii. In learning Haida stories directly from the elders, and from those recorded texts in ethnographies, Shaun finds insights into the past. Each encounter brings deeper understanding of Haida culture and images. "The stories," he maintains, "are our main art. If I can get good enough to portray the traditional stories, I'll consider myself a success."

One of Shaun's large argillite sculptures is based on stories of the mighty *tc A'maos* (meaning "tide-walker") or Sea Grizzly. A hybrid of sea and land, Sea Grizzly has the anatomical attributes of a bear combined with the large dorsal and pectoral fins of the killer whale. A Raven crest belonging primarily to families from Skidegate, Ninstints and Rose Spit, Sea Grizzly represents the strength and prowess of marine hunters. This supernatural creature is also described as having the power to assume many forms including a semi-submerged log or snag. Shaun's sculpture of Sea Grizzly conveys the power and strength of this giant creature.

For many First Nations people, to be a singer or a composer of songs is an expression of the sacred, and sometimes comes from or is inspired by supernatural encounters. Shaun is a keen drummer and singer who is still learning traditional songs and rhythms. He seeks inspiration for his music and for his carving through learning Haida. With guidance from his uncle James Young in Skidegate and language tapes made by his tsinii Stephen Brown of Old Masset, Shaun studies both dialects. He hopes through his experience he will pass his enthusiasm for Haida ways of knowing to his children:

I love to sing and read some of the old stories to my daughter, Shaunnay, and my son, Markus. My mom and my naanii Violet took my daughter out to the forest and taught her how to gather some of the medicines and how to put them together. They taught her the use of some of these medicines. That's what makes you Haida! That's how we can maintain the culture for future generations yet to come.

Shaun continues to create argillite art, exploring old and new forms. He also carves masks in fragrant woods, makes drums, and has experimented with engraving copper blades for ceremonial daggers. Carpentry may replace fishing for a while, but his goal is to create argillite sculpture as a full time artist. Being Haida holds tremendous significance for Shaun, and being an artist is a major part of that identity:

Using my own eyes, my own vision, I'm hoping to create art that will reflect old values through old and new stories for the generations coming after me. The future, as I see it, is to show the world that our Haida art form is not lost, but growing stronger. It will show that our people still have a connection to the land and sea of Haida Gwaii. Through my argillite art, I hope people will enjoy our stories, appreciate this rare stone that is so unique. I want people of the world to know that when they hold an argillite sculpture, they are holding a valuable piece of history. I want to be part of that history.

CHRIS RUSS
Naylanch

100: (above) Chris Russ carves wood, silver and argillite at his workbench.

101: (facing) Chris's *Raven Steals the Light* illustrates how Raven stole the sun from the supernatural Sky Chief, who kept it in his box. In a plot to steal the sun, Raven transformed himself into the child of the chief's daughter. The child cried incessantly and to appease him, his grandfather allowed Raven to play with the bright ball. One day he transformed back into his bird form, snatched the sun in his beak and flew through the smoke hole in the top of the house.

The round silver box turns slowly in his hands; Chris Russ scrutinizes every line on the engraved surface, rubs a polishing cloth once again over the cool metal. Gently he sets the box's argillite lid into place and suddenly it's no longer a precious jewellery container: it is a reflection into prehistory, a primordial time when all the world was in chaos and as dark as this stone. The jewellery box becomes more than a sculpture in silver and argillite — it is Raven on the cusp of bringing light into the universe.

Known by various names in Haida — *koyah* or *xuyaa, yaahl, nankilslas* or *nang kilsdlaas* (also written *nAñkî'lsLas*) — Raven is a principle figure in Northwest Coast creation stories. A trickster, shape shifter and magician, he is known for being lecherous, mischievous, greedy and voracious. Yet, to his credit, though not by his own design, Raven is responsible for creating Haida Gwaii and the mainland of the Northwest Coast. Near Rose Spit he uncovered a clamshell that contained the first humans who would eventually populate the earth. Though often it was not his intent but more as result of his antics as a thief, pillager, and schemer, Raven brought many essentials to humans: salmon, oolichan, fresh water and sunlight.

Chris has depicted that crucial moment in the Raven episodes when the great supernatural being transforms from a child back into a bird. Having stolen the sun from his grandfather's treasure box, he pauses to peer at the roof of Sky Chief's house, the round ball of light solidly in his grasp. Poised to escape through the longhouse's smoke hole, Raven gazes skyward to liberation. He is seconds away from seizing the orb in his mouth, making a dash for the opening, and introducing light to the world. From his bounty, he will fashion the moon and the stars to illuminate the night sky. Fittingly, light glints off the silver base, illuminating a split-representation design of the bird in full flight, the sun in his mouth.

Chris Russ knows dozens of Raven stories along with many others so fundamental to Haida oral traditions. He uses the main characters from the stories such as Wasgo (*suu sraa.n*) or Sea Wolf, Killer Whale, Bear Mother, Volcano Woman, and Shark Woman, incorporating different episodic elements from the rich descriptions he hears from elders or reads in books:

I've gone over the stories, learned the images that come from them, and practised them over and over. There are lots of stories I know and want to try to put into argillite, but I need to refine the images in my mind. I feel I need to get them perfect. I have to do it this way no matter whether I'm doing argillite, wood, gold or silver.

Some of the story characters find their way into his argillite art, but as he is quick to acknowledge, it's not so much that he applies the images to the argillite as it is the stone dictating what it wants to be:

Where do I get the idea for a certain piece? It takes a lot of study of the block itself. It takes me days of studying it — sometimes two or three days of just looking at the argillite. If I have a certain idea of what I want to do, and if it's not in the stone, then it won't come out to me. When the stone does tell me what it wants to be, it's usually a few more days of studying it, planning it once I figure the shape I'm going to carve.

I make the first cuts and the body inside comes to me. There's a form inside. The way I first see it is the way the animal looks in nature, then it's the design that comes. The characters are shape shifters, transformation is always happening, and I learn about it. This process doesn't happen easily, and if I force it, it won't come out right. The raven in that little jewel box came out right away, but it's not always like that.

Chris has been making these jewel boxes for several years. Small in scale but monumental in scope, the boxes reflect his quiet approach to the world. There's nothing flamboyant or hasty in him personally or in his artistic style. His voice is gentle, thoughtful; his art is elegant, meticulous in every detail. A man of few words and careful expressions, Chris creates forms that are graceful, yet the images themselves spring from his imagination, their movement frozen at the instant of critical exchange or transformation. Through his sculpture, Chris grants us insight into complex mythological themes and helps us to contemplate them with him.

From the Raven clan, Chris has received the name that originally belonged to his paternal grandfather, Willie Russ, Sr: *Naylanch*, which has several meanings: "Holler-from-Behind-the-House", "Noisy House" or "House-of-Noise". Chris' father is Reynold Russ, Chief *Iljawass*, the hereditary chief of Old Masset from the *maaman git'anee* Eagle clan. His mother, June Russ, is a member of the *Laxgibuu* (Wolf) clan and came from Kincolith (*Gingoix*), one of the four villages of the Nisga'a Nation. His grandmother, who is also Martin Williams' grandmother, was Marjorie (Barton) Williams; she used both the Wolf and Eagle crests. Among Chris's clan crests are Eagle, Wolf, and Killer Whale. The Nisga'a live on the mainland across from the Haida on the Nass River.

Chris comes from a family of artists — his brother, Ron Russ, and cousin Martin Williams are notable argillite carvers. His sisters Sheila Russ and Colleen Williams along with his younger brother, Irvin Russ, are weavers.

Ron and Chris began carving argillite about the same time, though Chris stopped for a while to travel. He returned to making sculpture in the mid-1970s and has been doing it full time since then. His children, Justine and Konrad, have shown interest in studying the family's lineage history and the traditional arts. These are interests he is eager to foster. Remembering how he started by learning tool-making in Claude Davidson's workshops and by watching other carvers, Chris is a willing teacher who hopes emerging artists will begin as he did, by learning to make their own tools along with studying traditional stories:

I enjoyed Claude; he was a funny guy and he made me laugh. He was also good at teaching about the tools and carving. Today, monumental poles are making a comeback. I can help by teaching other carvers how to make the tools. I will be alive in other people's poles because of what I taught in the tool-making course. If people remember your name as a teacher, you'll always be alive.

102: (upper facing) Chris's *Bear Prince Captures the Woman* lidded bowl illustrates the consequences of a princess who stepped in bear excrement and cursed the bear. In the forest she meets a handsome young prince who takes her back to his village and marries her. Her husband turns into a bear. She gives birth to half-bear children.

103: (lower facing) Chris has depicted Bear Mother riding on the back of a bear. He has rimmed the lid in copper and inlaid the bear's body with copper and abalone.

104: (above) Chris's *Raven Stealing the Sun* illustrates Raven's moment of contemplation before he takes his treasure and flies through the smoke hole of his grandfather's longhouse. His feathers were blackened as he flew through the smoke. After Raven stole the sun, he broke off pieces of the glowing ball to make the moon and the stars. Eventually he deposited the sun in the heavens, illuminating the world.

105, 106: (above) In Chris's sculpture of Raven finding the first humans in a clamshell on the beach, Raven's wings gently envelop the shell with its surprised men peering into their new world. In some stories, Raven nurtures his foundlings, and when they appear confused and aimless, he attaches sticky chiton shells to some of the men, transforming their male genitals to female ones.

107: (facing) The sculpture *Eagle Man* depicts a man in an Eagle headdress who is slowly transforming either from or into the supernatural bird. Eagle feathers have grown from beneath his arms.

Chris has taken inspiration from a variety of sources. Looking at the master carvers from the past that he's seen in museum collections, he admires the work of Tom Price, a contemporary of Charles Edenshaw, and Tom Watson, another artist who was a chief at Skidegate. Chris admires their intricate carving and attention to fine detail. "They were different from everyone else," he says, "like I am." The contemporary artists he holds in high esteem are Bill Reid and Robert Davidson. He appreciates their fine control of line and form:

I try to carve at a level somewhere between these artists rather than do the same as they have done. I'm aware of being different from other people in my art and in my personal life. I've always been alone and worked on my own. I study everything. If I need help, I go and look for it in many different places, but I don't often need help. I want to be recognized for my carvings and pass this knowledge on to my nephews.

In describing his own style, Chris says he too likes to be precise and attend to fine detail. He's particular about presenting his work. He plans a base for each sculpture and prefers not to do too many abalone or

110

108: Caught in a moment of transformation, Dogfish Woman with her high domed forehead, gill slits on cheeks and forehead, and asymmetrical shark's tail, reaches forward with human arms and hands. As with most Dogfish Woman images, she wears a large lip plug in the lower lip of her down-turned mouth.

mother-of-pearl inlays. "It takes away from what I see in the design," he says. "Inlays may look better to some patrons, but I don't feel that my style needs the extra embellishment." He tends to work small, but he values presenting monumental ideas that have feeling, presence and solid form. When he does add inlay to his argillite, he says it's usually for a very good reason.

For example, on the sculpture of Dogfish (*q'a.ad*) or Shark Woman, Chris's inlay on the shark's uneven-lobed tail draws the eye upward, just as the abalone inlay in the shark's lower lip indicates that this particular female has a labret: a disk in her lower lip distinguishing her gender, but also her high rank. Other inlays on her pectoral fins draw the eye to her human hands and arms under the fins, indicating that this is no ordinary dogfish (a variety of small shark found in Haida Gwaii), but a supernatural being in the act of transformation.

This sculpture illustrates the story of a woman who was taken by Dogfish to his home under the sea. There she saw that the dogfish remove their blankets and assume human form. The Haida call them *tsagan xaaydagaay* or "under water people". She stayed with the dogfish people for a long time and eventually she began growing fins on her arms and legs and transformed into Dogfish Woman. When she returned to her human village, she brought the dogfish crest to her family.

Though Chris considers himself an artist, he also thinks of himself as a student and in a very special way, as a parent of his sculpture:

For every piece I do, I'm being taught yet. I look at each of my pieces closely and sometimes it seems as if it's not shaped right. I look over and over a piece to see if it's finished. I feel when it's done. If it feels alive and warm — especially the smaller pieces — then it's done. If it feels cold, I know it wasn't finished; it usually doesn't sell right away.

My art's like a child: it grows up in my hands and then all of a sudden it's leaving home. When that happens, it's like part of my spiritual side leaving. And in return I get a piece of paper. I dream of getting some of my sculptures back, even if it's just to hold them for a day. They are my children; I brought them to life.

Chris Russ visualizes his argillite sculpture travelling outside Haida Gwaii, and to use his own metaphor, it is like sending a piece of himself to distant lands, other cultures. He imagines unknown people holding his sculptures, turning them over in their hands, seeing beyond the obvious to the deeper meanings contained in his forms. Like most artists, he wants people to appreciate his work on a personal level, but on another level he believes argillite sculpture has a much more important function:

When people hold my art in their hands, I want them to see that's me. The world is looking at me through my art. I am here. But on a bigger scale, argillite is keeping the Haida alive. The stories are important. That's what's keeping the art alive. By being an argillite artist, I'm doing something for the Haida Nation and the Nisga'a Nation. Without art, a nation will die. Artists can keep a nation alive — no matter what nation it is.

His soft voice and gentle spirit belie Chris Russ's fierce determination to make his contribution to keeping the culture viable and vibrant — one sculpture at a time. As the argillite works leave this artist's hands, they carry their own illumination of a people, a history and a land that are, by global standards, treasured.

MARTIN WILLIAMS

In much demand, Martin Williams' sculptures leave Haida Gwaii almost as soon as they are finished. This is not surprising. Since its inception during the first quarter of the 19th century, argillite art has been created solely for trade and sale to non-Haidas, mostly Euro-American sailors and merchants. As was true in the past, argillite sculpture produced in the 21st century is not for indigenous consumption but is intended for the global art market. Travelling to new places, taking residence in far-away homes or galleries, these pieces carry with them the cultural ethos of Haida Gwaii. Martin's sculptures convey more than simple messages to the outside world about his home or being Haida. He is a master of depicting stories that have been told for generations—stories funda-mental to Haida thought.

At our fingertips is his sculpture of Nanasimgat, who is also called *Gunarh* or *Gunarhnesemgyet* among Tsimshian speakers. The work illustrates the story of a man whose wife is abducted by a supernat-ural killer whale. As we reach for the artwork—Martin urges people to pick up his pieces—we anticipate a story so rich in thematic details and symbolism that it has fired human imagination across cultures and through the centuries. The figures capture the high drama of a husband's

bid to rescue his beloved from an undersea world where the powerful Killer Whale People, *Sgaana xaaydagaay*, live in villages that look like those inhabited by humans. In the story, Nanasimgat, following a series of prescribed tasks, successfully extricates his wife from Chief Killer Whale's longhouse and the couple return to their earthly village.

In some versions, the story begins with Nanasimgat's wife standing in the ocean shallows, washing the blood from a skinned white sea otter's pelt. Suddenly a supernatural killer whale abducts her and plunges below the waves to his village of longhouses under the ocean. In Martin's sculpture, the orca arches above her, holding her firmly between his pectoral fins; his tail sweeps between her legs, pinning her against his body. Nanasimgat, desperate to save his wife, clings to the killer whale's body with such force that he almost becomes transparent; his human body appears to merge into the great sea mammal's skin. The whale's violent motion and ferocity are exceeded only by Nanasimgat's sheer determination to succeed in this perilous undertaking.

People of the northern Northwest coast — the Haida, Tlingit, and Tsimshian nations — tell many versions of this Nanasimgat narrative cycle. Martin draws on Haida and Nisga'a stories when he creates episodes from the stories in argillite. Like his cousin Chris Russ, Martin claims this dual heritage because his maternal grandmother, Marjorie (Barton) Williams, was from Kincolith (*Gingoix*). Amos Williams of Old Masset is his tsinni.

A member of the Raven clan raised by his naanii and tsinii, Martin spent his early childhood in Old Masset, and then was sent off island to the residential school in Alert Bay, where he lived until 1969. "I'm a so-called survivor," he laughs. "I'm still here!" When he returned to Haida Gwaii, he began carving argillite in 1974 at the Yeltatzie household. He was the youngest to carve with them. Later he would be joined by other young men, among them Cooper Wilson, Mike Brown, and Gary Minaker Russ, who also would develop successful art careers:

I grew up with Mike Brown. We all carved together. It was a lot of fun. Sometimes we carved really big pieces at Percy Brown's house — Mike Brown's tsinii — but more often than not we were at the Yeltatzie house. You could stop by anytime; there was always somebody working on something. We just fed off each other, watched and learned from each other.

In that rich artistic environment, Martin recalls being influenced by George and John Yeltatzie, Ron Russ, and Donald Edgars. Martin feels a special debt to Fred Davis, who offered him solid critique about design and form, and also guided the young artist in learning traditional formline design:

I had to learn to draw first before I learned to carve. Fred taught me how to draw U-shapes and ovoids. I practised a lot and looked at old books that had

113

109: (facing) Martin's sculpture of Gunarh or Gunarhnesemgyet.

110: (above) Martin Williams.

114

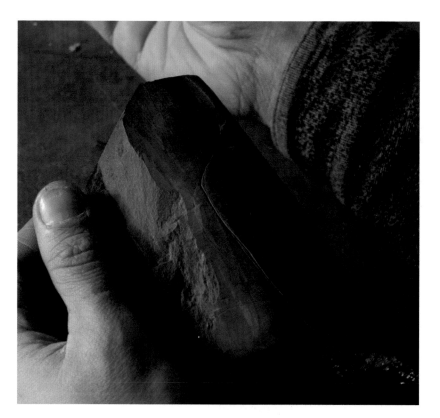

111: (above left) Detail of Gunarh, the hero holding on to the back of Killer Whale Chief so tightly that his body has merged into the orca's body and dorsal fin.

112: (above right) Martin has shown Gunarh's wife held firmly below the whale's head.

113: (right) Martin scribes a wing form on the side of a raw piece of argillite in preparation for carving.

pictures of our art. I was trying to figure it all out. I could see that our art is very structured—that's Haida—there are rules in the art that you need to follow to do the old style. Some of the contemporary guys figure they can go away from the rules, but you can't if you want to keep the art balanced.

Eventually, I learned how to put it together. One day it just clicked. I saw it; I put it all together. Once I could do that, I stopped drawing and went right into carving argillite. My first piece was a little frog medallion. I gave it to my naanii. You're supposed to give away your first piece; at least, that's what I've been told.

Until he found himself comfortable with formline design, Martin mostly carved pendants and medallions, but being around other accomplished argillite artists who were carving bowls and large sculptures soon inspired him to try three-dimensional sculpture. First referencing anthropologist Marius Barbeau's classic texts such as *Haida Myths* and especially *Haida Carvers in Argillite*, which he calls "our bible," Martin soon found himself studying Haida artists represented in museum collections. In particular, he was impressed by the work of a Skidegate carver, Isaac Chapman (or *Skilee)*, c.1880–1907. "I liked his realistic style, all his detail work, and especially the way he did big argillite bowls," he says. Poring over photos of other argillite artists' work, many whose identities were unknown or lost by ethnographers and photographers, Martin became acutely aware of individual stylistic signatures. He thought about the hand-made tools they used and discovered that he could follow in their footsteps by manufacturing tool sets specifically for his style of carving. He has always made his own tools from files and dental instruments. His appreciation for the art deepened as he incorporated new and old ideas into his own style.

For a while in the 1970s, Martin worked in Prince Rupert at the carving shed at the Museum of Northern British Columbia with Mike Brown and Hector Thompson, a Masset carver. In the early 90s, Martin worked alongside Cooper Wilson in Juneau at the Raven's Journey Gallery, carving argillite. He also learned to sculpt in wood, creating masks and daggers, and assisting master artist Jim Hart in carving two crest poles. Work in metals and wood interested Martin, but argillite remained his specialty:

I just kept coming back to argillite. Sure, it's not as clean as wood or even silver work, but I just love its flexibility. You can carve more detailed, delicate lines and forms. Argillite's unique in its origins and in Northwest Coast art. It's uniquely Haida. That makes being an argillite artist unique too.

Most guys start out in argillite, and then when they get good, they move on to wood and metal. And, you know, very few come back to argillite after they leave it, primarily because it's so dirty. I always want to carve argillite because I'm not confined by the medium. I can do work that you just can't do with wood or metal, or at least, if you tried to do something really detailed

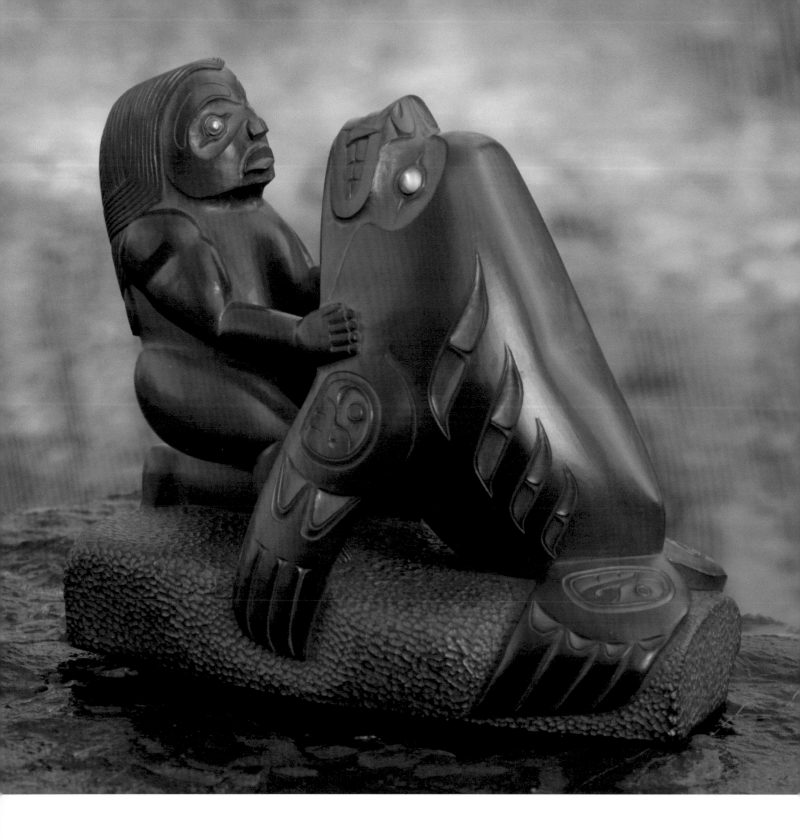

114: The story of Su'san, or Strong Man, comes to life in Martin's argillite sculpture illustrating the hero's superhuman strength. The man avenges his uncle by tearing in two the sea lion responsible for his death.

and flowing, it would be very tricky. There's so much you can do with argillite, so many finishes and shapes.

Martin did leave argillite carving for a few years to pursue another passion: preserving Haida Gwaii's environment. For 16 years he worked for the Haida Fisheries Program under the auspices of the Council of the Haida Nation in the "fisheries guardian" initiative that improves research knowledge about the aquatic populations of Haida Gwaii. In recent years, he has worked on the board of the Delkatla Wildlife Sanctuary in Masset, one of the few stopping places on the north-south coastal migration route for dozens of bird species. A committed environmentalist, he believes in holding people accountable for their interactions with the environment. "We all have to do all that we can to leave it for our kids." While he's committed to the wildlife sanctuary, he now considers himself "retired" from other work so he can devote all his time to carving argillite.

In this directed avocation, Martin's sculpture teaches people about intricate aspects of Haida stories and life. His argillite always refers to a story; he rarely does a single figure. By illustrating some stories, he points to the larger body of interrelated tales. For example, in illustrating the story of Su'san (also called *suu sraa.n* or *7waasru*), Martin had to consider that this name belongs to both Wasgo or Sea Wolf as well as to another cultural hero, the Strong Man. Su'san is actually a human who skins Wasgo, wears its skin, and thus assumes the power to perform super-human feats. Frequently, Martin will write his version of the story to accompany the sculpture when it leaves his hands. By choosing to illustrate one aspect of this narrative, Martin provides insights into the complexity of Haida thought:

I like to illustrate a story because it helps people understand our art a little better. I show them an abbreviated version of it so they can grasp a part of our history and our culture.

People who buy my art are buying some of me too. I enjoy carving stories that have a hero, like Su'san. That's artistic freedom: they see parts of the story the way I see it, my interpretation. I could do 10 versions of the same story and none of them would look the same even if they were illustrating the same episode. I like to leave people asking questions about what the figures mean. They will want to know what the story's about and how it relates to the Haida. When they know, then they can pass on an accurate interpretation of the story.

For example, in the documentation that accompanies his Su'san sculpture, he describes how the inspiration for it came from the story as told in three old northern Haida villages that are close to where he lives. His sculpture captures that moment in the story when Su'san takes revenge on a sea lion who killed Su'san's uncle. The vengeful hero demonstrates his supernatural strength by ripping the powerful sea mammal in two.

Understanding this fairly straightforward portrayal of this episode in the story, however, may not necessarily lead people towards an understanding of Martin's artistic process, which involves breathing complex ideas into black stone:

When I approach a piece of argillite, I usually have an idea in my head. I look at the chunk of stone and see if it matches my idea. I have to see it in my head before I start it, but I can picture it in my head only so far. Then I get to the point of roughing out the piece. It evolves as I start to figure out the details. I don't like to waste any of the stone. Sometimes I work out ideas in small pieces, and then try them again in larger pieces. It's important to me that the figures aren't rigid, that they're caught in motion.

The finishing is important too. I learned to do tool finishing from Fred Davis and Ron Russ. I like the tool finish because I like the texture of it and how it makes the figures look so natural, not like shiny and polished stone. I only use sandpaper when I'm finishing abalone for inlays. How it feels when you hold it is important. Argillite needs to be felt in order to be seen.

Sometimes it is hard to say a sculpture's done, to say 'that's enough.' I guess there's the temptation always to perfect the form, but sometimes you can spend too much time on a piece and it won't get any better.

Martin's love of carving argillite is matched by his love of relating the old stories through his art. Valuing and respecting his Haida heritage, he uses his art to tell the world about Haida Gwaii—his nation, its rich cultural history and its people. For Martin Williams, his argillite art conveys a sense of self, of place, of identity, but it also conveys his sense of obligation to the past and the future of Haida life and traditions:

As Haida artists, we're unique, distinct here in our own little world. There's not that many of us now, but we're starting to build our art, our traditions, our clan strengths. It's like those Su'san stories where the people shun the man, but he doesn't give up. He finds his own strength.

There are good lessons for our youth here: even if people discourage you, go after what you want. Don't give up. We're Haida. We should try to keep it that way. We can't lose that by being mistaken for or being absorbed into a "global community". As artists in this generation we're charged with keeping the traditions alive.

115: Martin's attention to detail is demonstrated in the elaborately braided hair of his muscular Su'san figure. From this view, the sea lion seems completely overpowered by the man's size and superhuman strength.

ROBERT VOGSTAD
Luptaagaa

116: Robert in front of his painting
We Are What We Eat.

"Robert Vogstad was an artist before he was born." Jolting and unexpected, this characteristically succinct statement is the opening line on Robert Vogstad's personal website. His sometimes self-effacing humour glosses over a lucid sense of self and purpose. Smiling, he elaborates on his artistic beginnings: "I started drawing in my mother's womb, with the light coming through her stomach. I'm pretty sure I remember those days." He pauses, savours the moment as his listener absorbs the implication; they laugh together. This may be Robert's way of creating a sense of immediate access to his innermost thoughts about his life as a Haida artist, the environment he inhabits, and the culture he celebrates with every breath.

Robert is a man balancing many features of his life. He takes pride in his dual ancestry. Tracing his paternal connection to a Norwegian family that arrived in Canada three generations ago, he counts a gold and silversmith who handcrafted fine jewellery among his 18th century ancestors. Arnfin, part of Robert's family name, means "Old Norse".

Robert is also part of an old Haida family whose heritage is deeply rooted in Haida Gwaii. His father, Larry Vogstad, and his mother, Mary Williams Vogstad, made sure that as a youngster, Robert would visit his Haida grandmother, Margaret Stanley Williams, every summer in Skidegate. From his *nuni* he learned about his Haida family's paternal connection to Yan (*yaan 'lanngee*) and their maternal connection to Naikoon (*nèekun* or *na7i kun*).

Robert was born in Haida Gwaii and is a Raven of the *K'yaanuu Slii* or Cod People clan; his crests are Raven, Grizzly Bear, Dogfish, Killer Whale, and Star. Later in life, while working as a Haida Gwaii Watchman living in the abandoned village of Skun Gwaii (*sran gwaay*) or Ninstints at the tip of Gwaii Haanas, Robert conducted tours and spoke with maritime visitors about Haida culture, life and ecology. He received the name *Luptaagaa*, meaning "yappy" or "the talkative one", from Captain Gold and his wife Bernice (whose Haida name is *Djadau Unn Koo Ding Uss*), two elders who lived at Skung Gwaii for that season.

For the first part of his life, Robert lived with his family away from Haida Gwaii, though, he says, "I was always drawn home by the art, the people, and the beauty of our islands. I believe the islands are a living entity. I call the islands *Naanii Gwaii*—Grandmother Islands."

As a youngster, Robert watched his older brother Larry carve argillite. "I was just hanging around and wondering what that black stuff was," he says. He watched Larry make pendants and had enough interest to try his hand at carving, though it didn't make a real impression on him at the time. "I was attracted then, but I really wasn't aware of what it was. I was curious, played with some argillite that he gave me, but I was very naïve."

When he was in his early 20s, Robert decided to further his artistic talents, which up to that time had been mostly self-taught, and enrolled in the Emily Carr Institute of Art and Design in Vancouver. There he studied painting and printmaking. "When I was in Emily Carr," he explains, "I was doing expressionism. I consider myself a neo-traditionalist."

Neo-traditional is not a term he applies lightly or confines to the paintings and prints he produced in the Institute; it's something he's given considerable thought to and believes about himself. He expressed the meaning of the term in an artist statement in connection with a show at the Alcheringa Gallery:

Today a resurgence of innovative concepts changes the face of the Northwest Coast art. Using traditional forms and stories that comply with non-traditional media is part of the innovation. Native artists that grasp onto modernity seek to express themselves in a new light. Lawrence Paul borrows from Salvador Dali's surrealistic world to express his own. Rick Bartow uses expressionism to transform man to animal in the moving moment of transformation. The important thing for us to remember is that we can break boundaries and surpass conformity and yet maintain the essential links to tribal roots. This is Neo-traditionalism.

At Emily Carr, Robert developed a unique painting style, layering effervescent pigments on canvases in a way that brought startling movement and realism to otherwise conventional Haida formline images. Pushing limits, yet resting comfortably in his knowledge and interpretations of identifiable Haida themes and symbols, Robert learned he could maintain an essential balance between the old and the new. He felt secure trying new things and using the phrase "because nobody's done it!" as a guiding principle for his twin artistic purposes: innovation and revitalization.

Released from predictable and conformist ideas of rule-bound northern Northwest Coast formline design, yet still respecting it, Robert's paintings express the transparency, tensions and transitions between culture and nature as a kind of landscape of the mind. In his extraordinary palette, neon meets natural pigment in depicting transformation images of life and death, the ordinary and the supernatural, imagination and crushing reality.

Robert renewed his interest in Haida art while attending Emily Carr. His campus was close to Bill Reid's studio on Granville Island and a stone's throw from the city's lively art gallery district. He took full advantage of his proximity to the cluster of Haida apprentices working in Reid's studio:

When I was at school, Bill Reid was down there at the same time. I just kept bugging him. I got back into Haida art by watching him and all my peers working with him: people like Garner Moody, Bill Bellis, and Tim Boyko. I was attracted again to Haida art and decided to pursue it even more. I was inspired by the monumental creations that Bill Reid and his apprentices were working on there.

Balancing his neo-traditionalist self-conception with his admiration for artists working in traditional and contemporary forms, Robert graduated from Emily Carr in 1989. It is a balance he has no trouble maintaining:

Being a neo-traditionalist, I believe in some of the things of the past and the things of the future, the present time. I'm a modern Haida. I use modern tools and I'm not going to limit myself, for example, to traditional colours, tools, or designs. I use them, but I'm not going to be limited by them.

I think Haida art from the very beginning was progressive and was always evolving. I like to think of it more as a spiritual experience rather than trying to make money by producing art. You know, when you try to make money at it, then your heart's not in the right place. You need experience to do it, to challenge yourself to explore things you haven't done — like portraying mythical creatures in a new way or working in different media.

Exploring as a means toward achieving spiritual and intellectual balance has become a way of life for this Haida artist. After finishing at Emily Carr, Robert began working seriously in argillite, at first doing small pieces. Carving flat pendants gave him limited satisfaction, so

122

117: Robert's sketch of three *gogit* or "land otter men" that he plans to carve in argillite. Traditionally the Haida believed that men could go mad after seeing or even hearing the sounds made by a land otter. Gogit (*ga gi.iid*) is often described as a wild, absent-minded spirit that demonstrates obsessive behaviour such as continually eating cod fish.

he progressed to carving bigger sculptures, seeking inspiration from his ancestors, in particular from the works of his grandmother's great grandfather, Simeon Stilthda or *skil kingaans* (c.1800–1889) and his pre-eminent contemporaries working at the turn of the 19th century: Charles Edenshaw (1839-1920), John Robson (1846–1924), John Gwaytihl (c.1820–1912), and Amos Kit Elswa (n.d.).

After living for four years in the Okanagan Valley in the interior of British Columbia, Robert moved to Victoria, where he met and found a mentor in Haida master carver Louis (Junior) Widen, brother of Richard Widen:

Prior to moving to Victoria, I had a dream one night about a gogit, *a Haida wild man. In the dream he was riding a bicycle and laughing at me, sort of teasing me in the gentle way that the Haida do. It was such a vivid dream that I quickly drew it as soon as I woke up. When I moved to Victoria, I was introduced to Junior and though I'd never met him before, he looked familiar. He just laughed at me and said, "Some people call me the gogit!" It was the man in my drawing, the man in my dreams.*

He taught me a lot. Everything I know about argillite carving, I learned from Louis Widen. He taught me a different perspective on using subjects, to make them appear more realistic in the tradition of Simeon Stilthda. He taught me everything from patience to tool-making. Junior showed me techniques for meticulous inlays, how to hold my chisels, and how to make my own tools from files. This was invaluable. At that time, he was moving away from carving and more into shamanism, so I got some tutoring in those ideas as well. I was really there to learn about art, but I was a good listener.

Robert began to augment painting and printmaking with carving argillite. As always, his thoughts for any artwork began with drawing. Filling dozens of sketchbooks with literally hundreds of sketches, Robert worked out page after page of complex relationships, design details, and intricate ideas, visually exploring the multifaceted spiritual ecology of Haida thought. Some of the drawings evolved into paintings; some became the basis for sculpture in wood or argillite. Going from two-dimensional work to three-dimensional sculpture brought Robert new challenges and new ways of thinking:

It is a different mindset. But as the old carvers say, "If you can draw it then you can carve it." You just have to see the picture in your head. You have to draw continually until you can carve the image. You just keep drawing and drawing until you get that persona of the animal; you accept the challenge of presenting the form the way it wants to be. I might do 10 pages of drawings until I perfect the design.

When I begin an argillite piece, I look at the rock, the stone, and then it usually dictates what it wants to be—even if you don't see it, the presence is there. You have to look at it and get familiar with the argillite and it will speak to you about what it wants to be. You don't want to force something that won't come naturally.

Argillite presents different problems than wood, because when you start to carve, something can break. You then have to think more about how to continue, to save it, to compensate for the change in the stone. This is not a negative thing if it breaks or chips: it just tells you how its spirit wants you to go. We have a spirit teacher; I listen to that voice and am sensitive to it. Sometimes I hear the voice of my great great great grandfather, Simeon Stilthda.

When I let go of a sculpture, I trust that the spirit of that carving will find the right person who will love it and take care of it. So I think of that. Sometimes I mourn my carvings when I let go of them. It's like giving away part of my spirit, especially if they've been around for a while.

From his time in Victoria, there are two small sculptures in a private collection: *Wolf with Raven*, a small sculpture that depicts a wolf gently holding the bird close to its belly; and *Sqaana*, a porpoising supernatural Killer Whale with a human face in its blowhole. These are early pieces, simple explorations in form and style.

In another sculpture, *Shaman and Thunderbird*, the subject is more complicated in form and in meaning. Caught in the moment of transformation, a shaman shifts in the blink of an eye from his human persona to his supernatural entity as the ceremonial blanket surrounding him becomes the feathers and body of the great bird. His coming and going are shrouded in mystery, frozen in time. Inlaying the bird's eyes with cool jade and the shaman's eyes with glowing amber, Robert stepped outside of convention, eschewing abalone for the inlays, and instead, selecting stones that echoed lively colours from his palette.

118: (lower left) In one of his first attempts at argillite sculpture, Robert carved this small Wolf with its large curling tail holding a small raven.

124

119: (lower right) *Sqa'na* or supernatural Killer Whale is sculpted with traditional formline designs as it rides above waves that look more painted than carved. The movement and texture of the water are reminiscent of Robert's brush techniques.

120-122: (facing) *Shaman and Thunderbird.* The shaman has transformed from a human into a supernatural being.

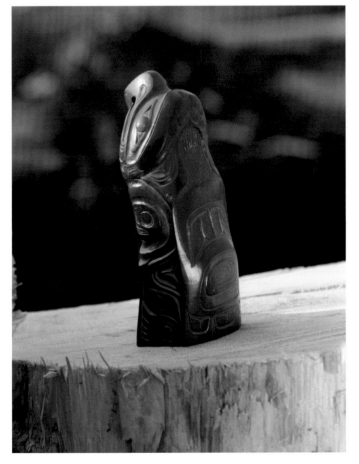

Finding and maturing his artistic voice, Robert has developed a new
level in his sculpture while maintaining a sense of innovation and revitalization in his painting. His style in both carving and painting has
evolved, become confidently far-reaching in experimentation. In some
ways, he has combined both disciplines—creating paintings with sculptural dimensions and sculptures with painterly vision.

In his paintings, he uses traditional two-dimensional formline designs
to create human and animal subjects, but animates them by showing
them in three dimensions, blurring the distinction between realism
and conventional portrayal of Haida images. The planes of his carved
wooden masks are precise and structured, yet they are overlaid with
exuberant brushstrokes of vibrant paint, recalling the work of master
carver John Gwaytihl. When it comes to argillite sculpture, Robert's use
of tool finishing and serrated gouges brings to mind his expressionistic

123: (facing) *Lazy Son-in-law in the Wasgo Skin.* In this complex sculpture, Wasgo's dorsal fin has been punned as Raven's long sharp beak. In some stories, Raven escapes from inside the body of a killer whale by pecking a hole through the tip of the orca's dorsal fin.

124: (above) Wasgo's toothy jaws have been realistically inlaid with dog salmon teeth.

125: (left) Face of the dead son-in-law who wore Wasgo's skin and assumed supernatural powers. The texturing strokes detailing the hero's hair are similar to the swift bold brushstrokes used by 19th century master carver John Gwaytihl.

painterly style and the short jabs of his loaded brushes. Robert strives to add movement, pure form and space around his sculptures. "I like to make them more free-flowing, more Rodin-like," he says.

In his sculpture of *Lazy Son-in-law in the Wasgo Skin*, Robert brings the monstrous image of a snarling Sea Wolf to life. There is no question that this is a supernatural creature of great power, for he has captured a mammoth killer whale and placed it in the curl of his great tail. Wasgo's dorsal fin is visually punned as a sharp-beaked Raven's head. The lower back of Wasgo has been laid open to reveal a human face, eyes closed in death.

In this small but monumental sculpture, Robert illustrates the dramatic narrative of a man who has been shamed by his mother-in-law for being lazy and not doing enough to help his village in a time of famine. Secretly, the man captures Wasgo, skins it and assumes its supernatural hunting prowess. After he dons the skin of Wasgo, the man has the ability to capture whales and bring them anonymously to the villagers. His mother-in-law, claiming she is a powerful shaman, takes credit for the fortuitous arrival of food. When Wasgo eventually dies in a final effort to replenish the starving village, his body washes ashore with many whales. When the villagers cut Wasgo open, they see the son inside the skin and learn the truth. Horrified, the mother-in law dies of guilt and shame. It's an old story, balanced with new vision.

Robert honours the old, celebrates the new, all the while wary of the reality of a world threatened with depletion; it is a message that he carries to his children Josef, Rebeka, and Twyla. In one painting, *We Are What We Eat*, Robert portrays a swirl of salmon figures. Inside each one is a different figure: "There's a bear in the salmon, a human in the salmon, an eagle in the salmon and then a raven in the salmon. It's a genetic link. I believe in the spirits of the past salmon." Extending the metaphor, Robert sees himself linked—past and present—to the spiritual, ecological, and cultural genome of Haida Gwaii. Balancing tradition and innovation, Robert Vogstad carves and paints that others may understand *Naanii Gwaii*.

129

126: (facing) Wasgo is so large that he captures orcas and carries them in his huge curling tail.

GARY MINAKER RUSS

Walking into a collection of Gary Minaker Russ argillite sculptures is like reading a book of ancient Haida stories: there is a common denominator in their epic quality, with narrative themes and images that impart a depth and complexity that seems inexhaustible. No two sculptures are alike, yet there is an interrelationship in the wide-ranging subjects. These are Haida stories, portrayed with all the concentration of symbols that can be envisioned or imagined in stone.

Gary's work is at once powerful and subtle. His organic forms tease the viewer's mind and provoke questions: Who is this? Why are they doing that? What are we supposed to understand from this image? When did this take place? Where is it happening? How did he do that? These are questions that Gary wants his viewers to ask about his sculptures, and the answers bring us nearer to this artist and closer to his culture. This is part of Gary's reason for being an artist.

Gary Minaker Russ is passionate about carving argillite: "It's all I ever wanted to do." The fifth of nine children in the family of Harold Minaker and Eleanor Russ, Gary comes from an impressive family of well-known argillite carvers: his brother Ed Russ (1953–2006), whose Haida name was *Gitajung*; Ed's wife Faye Russ; his cousin Ron, and Ron's son Marcel Russ; and his cousin Chris Russ. He is also related to argillite artists Martin Williams and Mike Brown. Born in Old Masset, he is from the Eagle clan. Eagle, Sculpin, Frog, and Black Whale are his crests.

Gary considers his style a unique blend of what he has developed on his own and what he learned from his brother Ed and his sister-in-law, Faye:

They were the best argillite carvers I've ever known. I was a teen when I went to live with them—at first I was sort of a live-in babysitter. When they moved to Powell River, it was a huge learning experience for me. As my teachers, they first taught me by showing me how to sell art and deal with people. I learned how to be prepared for the marketplace and not be turned off by it.

Then Ed taught me more about argillite carving by letting me rough out and shape some of his pieces. Both of them did extremely detailed and fine work. Ed and Faye both drilled it into me that I had to know the stories if I was going to be a Haida artist. I did learn the stories—from books and from Faye. They taught me to first know the stories, and then the images will come.

Gary learned these fundamental lessons well. His meticulous attention to detail and his fine tool finishes echo the work done by Faye Russ, one of the few female argillite carvers, who created flawless sculptures with precise cross-hatching and unique shapes. She herself studied with the well-known Skidegate artist Rufus Moody (1923-1998), holder of the Order of Canada, who was a prolific carver and who mentored many

127: (above) Gary Minaker Russ.

128: (facing) Gary's *Su'san,* or Strong Man, is shown wearing the skin of Wasgo as he struggles with his prey, a killer whale.

132

129: (above left) The human face of Strong Man.

130: (above right) The skin of Wasgo completely envelops the man's human body. Gary's composition is filled with the vitality and exertion of the underwater fight between the supernatural hero Su'san and the orca.

131: (upper facing) *Wasgo and Killer Whale* plate (1975) by one of Gary's teachers, Faye Russ. The precision of her cross-hatching and the dynamic three-dimensional effect of her low-relief carving give this plate a jewel-like quality.

132: (lower facing) *Double-finned Supernatural Shark.*

young Haida artists. In turn, Faye trained her husband to carve. Starting his career in 1972, Ed quickly became known for intricacy and innovation in his sculptures, as well as for his fine tool finishing—qualities that he felt would enhance the buyer's appreciation of argillite sculpture. Ed was able to pass on these concepts to his apprenticing younger brother. Gary adopted these ideals as his own:

I like to do tool finishing rather than polishing my work. It takes a lot longer, but it looks more natural. I like to encourage people to pick up my pieces, to hold them. It brings the owner closer to my sculptures. You can feel what you can't see. Edges, angles, corners become more apparent and you can become more involved with the sculpture.

For a short time, Gary worked in the logging industry and cod fishery as he continued to develop his artistic skills. At that time he carved mostly small pieces. A major turning point in his life came in the 1980s when he was logging in Naden Harbour: "I lost five or six friends to logging accidents and alcohol. That helped me make up my mind in a hurry to be a carver, and to be clean and sober."

In 1982, he began carving larger, fully dimensional sculptures and further developing his own style that he now considers "very different" from Ed and Faye's style. *"Pipes That Won't Smoke; Coal That Won't Burn* helped me a lot—in fact it started a whole new generation of carvers interested in argillite after they saw that book."

Part of developing his own style meant studying the work of past argillite artists in museums in Prince Rupert, Vancouver and Victoria. Ironically, he notes, "When I lived on the Charlottes, I never got to see much of the old Haida art. I had to leave in order to see more." In particular, he made frequent visits to the Royal British Columbia Museum's Reif Collection, where he grew to admire the work of Haida carvers from the 1870s and 1880s such as Charles Edenshaw and especially Isaac Chapman. His admiration for past masters and the quality of their art is always foremost in his mind:

Sometimes my admiration of the older carvings consumes me. My "mind power" comes from them. The ideas they put into argillite drive me. If I could live another 100 years I might be on their level. I know the quality and what it takes; it's a long way for me to get there.

I'm at somewhat of a disadvantage, though, because they were living what they were carving. That's a little bit of an edge. I carve based on what I read and see and hear from the elders. Some parts of the Haida experience may be missing. They carved from the heart. We carve from the mind, from memory.

133, 134: *Thunderbird and Killer Whale.* Gary's sculpture shows the Raven crest of the huge supernatural eagle-like bird that consumes orcas the way eagles feast on salmon. In this context, some Haida called killer whales "salmon of the Thunderbird". The colossal bird resembles an eagle except that it has a beak that recurves into a toothed mouth. According to some stories, this creature could create thunder by clapping its wings, and lightning would flash from its eyes. This is an unusual sculpture for this artist, for Gary rarely uses inlays in his work.

135: (above) *Blind Halibut Fisherman.*

136: (upper facing) The blind fisherman, with his elaborately detailed hair and ceremonial clothing, holds a catlinite halibut hook and a fish club. Gary designed the halibut hook to be detached from the sculpture and worn as a pendant.

137: (lower facing) Using low relief, the artist has carved a wraparound halibut design on the brim of the stylized woven cedar-bark chief's hat. Between the formlines, the warp and weft of the hat are visible. As it appears in nature, the halibut is shown with two round eyes on the same side of its head, a large curving gill, and a long diagonal mouth that extends from the top of the hat's brim to its outer edge.

Combining heart and memory with innovative artistic concepts, Gary creates argillite sculptures that consistently challenge the viewer. In sculptures that are massive, he incorporates elaborate details that demand closer inspection. Though his admiration for the works of the past is strong, his own creations are not slavish copies or mere re-workings of older sculptures. He revisits ancient stories with a fresh vision. While his images may be novel, Gary's primary interest is in being true to the stories and to give others insights into Haida thought:

In the old days, artists were only allowed to carve their own crests. I carve argillite with Eagle stories from my family, but I carve other Haida legends as well. I will carve a certain image only if I know the entire story—and I'll avoid doing anything if I don't know it. It's the only way to make a good sculpture.

The intricacies of the story seem to show up in the carving; I don't necessarily know them ahead of time. That's why I only carve single figures or single episodes from the stories. I don't mix elements from different sources because it won't make sense. It may look good to someone who doesn't know, but it won't mean anything to a Haida who knows the stories. If I appeal to the market rather than being true to myself, then people aren't going to learn about our culture.

In one complex sculpture, *Blind Halibut Fisherman*, Gary depicts the story of the man who managed to outsmart Raven's quest to steal his fishing bait. Two-thirds of the sculpture represent a woven cedar bark hat upon which the sightless fisherman sits wearing a ceremonial button blanket, fish club in one hand, and a catlinite, bone and abalone halibut hook in the other. Around the brim of the hat, Gary has wrapped the transparent formline design of a halibut.

In another sculpture, he freezes the extraordinary moment when a supernatural man transforms into an eagle. The man's head is being engulfed by an eagle headdress, and on the verge of amalgamating the bird's skull and its sharply curved beak with the human's face. Feathers are advancing down the man's neck and shoulders, and surrounding his chest. His arms are becoming feathered, spreading wing-like beneath an eagle dance blanket; his dancing apron is transforming into an eagle tail. Claws are shown emerging from the tops of his bare feet, soon to alter them completely into the eagle's powerful talons.

Gary's sculptures rarely incorporate inlays, relying instead on sculptural forms and implied movement to convey visual impact. While his subjects are based in his well-versed understanding of Haida thought and culture, he approaches the stone reverently, with respect for a higher power that guides his artistic endeavours, trusting that the stone, the story, the image, the act of carving, and the eventual owner are inti-

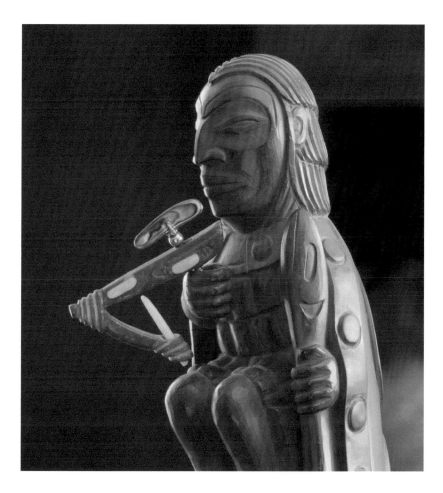

mately interrelated by spiritual forces beyond his own comprehension. It's a spiritually and physically demanding process, but understanding this dynamic helps him let go of a sculpture after he has spent weeks working on it, sometimes carving 10–12 hours a day:

Many of my sculptures originate with the stone telling me what to do. Sometimes it's as if the pieces are carving themselves and I'm just watching the stone do all the work. The argillite knows what buyer it wants to go to. Sometimes I can even imagine the buyer's face. I can do a carving with a collector in mind and personalize it for a certain buyer, but it seems that when I finish the sculpture, the carving just sells itself. It tells me where it wants to go.

It's not about the people or the price; it's about the carving picking a good home where it will be appreciated. That's how I learned to let go of my work.

138: (facing) Next to his signature and the date of the piece, Gary often writes a full explanation of the subject. On the bottom of this piece he has inscribed: "Supernatural Man who married the Eagle King's daughter wearing an eagle blanket with frog border and eagle dance apron giving him the power to transform into the Eagle."

139: (above left) On the reverse of this sculpture, feathers are beginning to grow from the man's body, wings are forming on the underside of his arms, and his feet are becoming eagle talons. Gary has frozen in argillite the actual moment of the supernatural man's transformation into Eagle.

140: (above right) A detailed examination of the man's head reveals that the feathers of the eagle headdress are merging with the feathers forming on the man's neck and shoulders.

141, 142: (above, upper facing) Gary's sculpture *Bear Mother in a Canoe* illustrates an episode in this long story. Bear Mother, a high-ranking human woman, married a prince, only to find when she went to live in his village that he was a supernatural being who could transform into a bear. In some stories, she is rescued by her brothers; in other accounts, she returns home with her husband and their half-human, half-bear offspring. In this sculpture, she and her brother travel in a traditional Haida cedar canoe. Gary has carved the fine details of their hair and cedar bark rain cloaks. The steersman peers over his shoulder as he pushes the canoe with a red catlinite paddle. In front of his knees, a prestigious chief's hat rests on a bentwood box. Bear Mother wears a large labret and holds a catlinite copper—both symbols of her high rank and great wealth. In the prow of the canoe, two young bear cubs comfortably huddle, watching for the journey's destination. Gary has carved a raven formline design on the sides of the canoe in high relief.

143: (lower facing) Gary Minaker Russ.

Gary works within strict ethical and artistic guidelines that he's set for himself. He won't do copies of his own or others' work, nor will he do the same theme twice. Most of the images he creates haven't been done before. Believing in the veracity and power of his own visual thinking, he makes his interpretations as unique as possible—"so they will be too much work for others to copy," he laughs. Using the same reasoning, he says he would find it hard to imitate what others are doing. Gary believes some Haida themes are overly exploited, such as the various depictions of Raven finding mankind in a clamshell. He simply won't be driven by the art market or by gallery owners' preferences:

When we work to the demands of the marketplace, we aren't allowed to drift out of conventional thinking and expand minds. In the late '80s until the early '90s, it was difficult for Haida carvers to do anything different. Galleries wanted us to be "traditional". I was disappointed in the touristy seasonal approach that the marketplace seemed to take. I did some soapstone sculptures and my private buyers loved them, but the galleries wouldn't touch them. I kept saying, "we're carvers, not commercial artists," but it will take a long time for them to wrap their minds around this idea.

It takes courage to make bold statements. Gary does this both with words and through his art. Assertive about his identity as a Northwest Coast artist, he hopes to inspire the next generation through his art and by his philosophy of honouring the past while being true to himself.

Gary Minaker Russ feels as much responsibility in being Haida as he feels pride. For him, it is a matter of legacy, one that he hopes to pass on to his sons Evan and Braden. While Gary doesn't pressure them to do visual art, he hopes that they will benefit from his knowledge as much as they benefit from his profession. As he looks to the history of ideas in Haida thought, he's keenly aware of his place as an artist in this century and of what he strives to pass on to the next generation:

To be born Haida and to have the ability to carve makes me one of the luckiest people in the world. It's an honour; it means everything to me. Artists are the lucky ones in our culture because, now that there are only about 4,000 Haidas in the world, we are part of keeping our heritage alive. It's a responsibility we can fill by carrying on the legends and stories of our culture through being exact and honest in their portrayal. When there are less of us, it means more to the world. We can't always think of this huge responsibility because it would slow us down. There's a lot to do. It's true, it's a burden—but it's also a blessing.

MARCEL RUSS

144: Marcel with his wife Lori, whom he calls his "muse".

Marcel Russ invites people not only to see his art but also to think about it, for in the thinking they will reach a deeper understanding of his life, his goals, and his philosophy. A natural teacher, he brings personal insight and life experience to everything he does, whether it's instructing a class of youngsters in the finer points of Haida art or dance, writing story books for children and adults, or creating an argillite sculpture.

He is a man in motion, continually thinking about and attracted to ideas about transformation. This is a common theme in Marcel's art, but it is also the focus for self-reflection about the changes in his own life, as well as the changes he believes he can contribute to his culture and his nation. Marcel sees himself ever growing, ever exploring the range of his personal expression, ever expanding his curiosity and expertise. And—as he frequently punctuates his descriptions about what he's doing—he's having fun.

Making art is as natural to Marcel as breathing. As a child he lived in Victoria with his mother, Lorraine Edgars, and later moved to Vancouver to live with his father, the noted artist Ron Russ. He began carving argillite at age eight. When Ron was out of the house selling his artwork, the young Marcel would pick up his father's tools:

I knew what I was going to be right from that point on. It was to be an artist. When I did my first little crest pole—it replicated one my dad had done—I used some of his tools and broke all his jeweller's blades. My dad was mad and happy at the same time. He was proud of my work. He wanted me to learn how to do three-dimensional sculpture right from the start.

At nine, Marcel began carving wood. He gave his first piece carved out of yew wood—a supernatural man transforming into Hawk—to the son of his uncle Chris Russ, a master carver and a major influence in his life. Moving on to carving more traditional pieces such as masks and headdresses, he gained an appreciation for different carving media:

I went back and forth from wood to argillite. I fell in love with argillite right away. It's the versatility of the material itself. For me, argillite was the one material that was capable of holding my ideas; it would do exactly what I envisioned in my mind. It was the one material that was able to do it. I tried with wood, but there are certain limitations to wood that argillite doesn't have—especially when I want to do really fine details.

At age 13 Marcel returned to Haida Gwaii to live with his tsinii and naanii, Reynold and June Russ. "The house in Vancouver was getting a little crowded," he laughs, "so I went home and helped my grand-parents." The rest of the family eventually joined him and moved into cousin Bruce Brown's house. There he was exposed to intense artistic activity which he describes as "one of the most super-creative times in my life." This period of growth moved Marcel from apprenticeship into maturity as he reached for his own artistic goals. That sometimes meant that his innovative spirit ran against the grain of the more senior artists who were his principle teachers:

Fred Davis, Martin and Vern Williams, Chris Russ, and of course, my dad were all carving in the basement of Bruce's house. They let me join them. We had a real studio going there, all carving together, learning from each other and feeding off each other. They were my teachers, and though I respected all of them, there soon came an ongoing struggle between us. I think I frustrated a lot of people at that time. They were doing really traditional things and I was beginning to move away from that, creating brand new stuff—within certain parameters, of course.

Some of them, especially my father, would say, "That isn't Haida—this is Haida!" but I finally got brave enough to do some things on my own. I felt I had to be respectful of the old styles and build on them, but still be creative and free to do what inspired me.

When some of the older carvers said, "No, you can't do that; no, you can't do this," it just put into my mind, "Yes, it can be done. Just because you can't do it doesn't mean I can't do it!" So I went and did things my way. It was just frustrating for everybody. But now I'm getting to that point in my life where I look at what I did then, and even my early teachers now appreciate it. I just say to myself, "Wow! You can be creative and original."

At such a young age, Marcel's advanced artistic sensibilities and wood carving skills were quickly noted, and he joined his father Ron and master carver Jim Hart working on a large crest pole for Yan. The experience was varied and rich and not limited to doing art. It was also a time of growing political awareness. "I left the pole carving project to go protesting against people who were fishing without permission off North Island," he says. During this time other events also influenced his career as a young artist, not the least of which was meeting renowned Haida artist Bill Reid:

Bill was there for a few weeks. I think he kinda grew fond of me because he would tell me stories and spent some time showing me things about wood-carving. He made some drawings to show me about pull-blades and he taught me about heating up and bending blades to make curved knives.

At this time Marcel expanded his artistic interests beyond sculpture. When his cousin Delbert Russ moved to Masset, he taught Marcel to paint canvases. "I isolated myself for about three years, just focusing on drawing and painting. I did that until I burnt out because I used to do it too much. And then I got into silver and mixing it with argillite."

145, 146: With fondness for combining silver and argillite, Marcel has engraved episodes from the primordial Raven Travelling stories on the sides of this round silver box. He carved the argillite base with a split-raven design and the lid with Raven's clamshell surrounded by the first men emerging from its interior.

147: (facing) Marcel has carved many monumental crest poles. On this one, a shaman holding circular rattles wears a shark headdress. The shark's uneven lobed tail rises above its domed forehead. Both the shark and the shaman have gill slits on their cheeks. Below the shaman is Frog, whose tongue extends over the forehead of a grizzly bear. The bear embraces another frog and they exchange tongues.

Ron encouragingly provided the impetus and the tools for Marcel to learn silverwork. It was the beginning of a serious passion for combining both media, something that he successfully continues in his current work:

I remember one day I was watching my father working with silver and argillite. He got annoyed with me because I was staring so hard at his hands while he was working. He was leaving to play golf, so he just threw me a piece of metal and said, "Here you go. The tools are there, the block's there!" I was so happy; I jumped on the engraving block and started carving away. Later on I got my own tools and a block of my own. It was fun just exploring my creativity.

When he was 18, Marcel left Haida Gwaii with the intention of "heading east" to find new markets for his art. He never got past Prince Rupert. Instead, he started a family. Though he continued to create art, it was not profitable. He says ruefully, "I stayed in Rupert for 10 years trying to do art in a place that was, at that time, in decline. Eventually, I couldn't give away my art, much less make a living doing it." He made a decision to go to Vancouver and soon connected with a cousin, Andy Williams, who took him to a carving studio in the Gastown area of the city. Another young Haida artist, Jay Simeon, was working there.

They let me watch them for a while, and then they invited me to carve with them. I started teaching Jay a few things about doing sculpture. I told him, "Ask me any question you want." I started showing him little things to improve his work. He was like an amazing sponge; he learned so incredibly fast and then just blossomed. Then it moved to a point where we were learning from each other. I had a lot of fun then, carving and playing basketball with him. Jay and I became more like brothers than friends.

Marcel's Vancouver years began on a promising note, and his work soon found its way into galleries and collections from Haida Gwaii to Arizona, from the West Coast to New York. Success, however, had its price. City life and urban pressures soon affected his health and lifestyle choices. He credits Jay with helping him in a time of personal challenges. "He stood by me and helped me out," Marcel says appreciatively. "Vancouver wasn't the place for me; it got my name out there, but it was dragging me down. I had to leave."

Before leaving Vancouver, however, he was introduced again to a childhood acquaintance, Lori McFadyen, whose Ojibwa family had known his own Haida family during his early growing up years in the city. Lori is an artist in her own right; a leatherworker and weaver, she is also learning to carve and paint. They connected spiritually and artistically, and eventually were engaged. Plans to move east changed after a vacation in Haida Gwaii. In December 2005 they made a joint decision

to return to Marcel's island home and make a life together. It's a decision they've never regretted, for together they found opportunity and tranquility in an environment that fosters creativity. In their island home, he set up a studio and began to carve argillite and wood.

One of the first pieces he completed there was *Shaman Torturing a Witch*, a monumental argillite sculpture that is profoundly autobiographical in content. The image is rooted in old stories about shamans or doctors who cured people of spells and curses, sometimes persecuting the witchcraft perpetrator. In Marcel's sculpture, the shaman, wearing the mask of his supernatural helper, Octopus, grasps the witch by the hair. He has used a club to break the witch's legs, thus immobilizing the evildoer.

There are two figures in this sculpture—both are me. There are a lot of emotions in the figures: fear and power, strength and determination. It represents the old me and the new me. It's a battle. The shaman or medicine man part of me is winning a personal battle, facing personal challenges and overcoming them. This image is coming from my own way of seeing things, of meeting life head-on. It's my story. I'm writing my own legends in art and in the books I'm doing.

I'm creating my own stories as I walk through life with my art. People are slowly understanding that. That's how we were as a nation, as a people. We have our legends and stories, but if you look at old Haida art, it was day-to-day things they experienced and carved into their art. That's how we wrote things down—with our art.

Powerful images like *Shaman Torturing a Witch* don't just happen. It is a process that Marcel articulately describes as bringing together an idea and a piece of argillite. Before he begins carving, he tries to imagine the stone's internal structure and plans how he will release the image from the argillite. Sometimes he'll begin by sketching a design for a sculpture, getting a rough idea of what he would like to carve, but the result may be completely different from his drawings. "It may be the same story as my drawing, but what's inside the stone always comes out. When I'm carving, I have to bend the images this way and that so they will fit properly." It's a process he learned from his father and has refined through years of experience:

I start by breaking off the pieces of the rock in my mind's eye—by taking it apart and twisting things on the inside of the argillite. Before I cut it, I have to visualize what's inside it first, not what I can draw on the outside. I can draw anything I want on the outside, but I found a real good key to sculpting is to be able to envision what's on the inside, the stuff you can't see. It's in there.

148: (facing) *Shaman Torturing a Witch.* The shaman has broken the witch's leg with his club. He grasps her by the hair, confident that he has overpowered the shrieking evildoer. This sculpture has deep personal meaning for Marcel, and he has used a powerful visual metaphor to symbolize the struggle to conquer his own life challenges.

149: (below) The back of the sculpture shows the life-like representation of the Octopus helper's body with its writhing tentacles. In Haida stories, some octopus (also called devilfish) live in human-like societies under the ocean.

You have to be able to follow the image like a tentacle of an octopus that goes through the sculpture and comes out the other side. You're following the vehicle that goes through the piece itself. That was the hardest part of my training; it's what my father taught me to do.

When it comes to argillite, I'll let the piece do the talking. That's why I find it really tough to take specific commissions. Someone will tell me what he wants and I have to say, "Well, I'll see what I can do." Then I'll get a piece of argillite and it might be a completely different idea of what the person wants. I have to tell them, "Just give me a general idea of what you want: a sculpture or a bracelet or a pendant. Let me do what I do best—create brand new, out-of-the-ordinary things—give me that freedom." They'll be happy with the result as long as they give me that. I've been free all my life and that's where I work from best.

Marcel's well known for carving pendants in argillite, though they're so fully three-dimensional that they're not so much pendants as wearable sculpture. One such piece he carved for Lori, whom he describes

as his "muse". The pendant depicts Creek Woman or *Djila'qons*, ancestress of the Haida Eagle clans. Marcel says, "She's the only person that Raven truly loved besides himself. She was his first, his only true love. I'm a Raven from the *Słangna 7laanaas* clan. I gave it to my wife." The pendant reveals Marcel's love of his ancestral heritage and his ability to translate the stories into argillite.

While the pendant's image remains deeply personal, the story of Creek Woman (sometimes called Volcano Woman among the Tsimshian) is a favourite among the Haida. She appears often in the stories and, according to Marcel, "is the mother of all beings walking around." In one story, young men throw Frog, an animal sacred to Djila'qons and sometimes referred to as her child, into a fire in a thoughtless act of cruelty. In revenge, this supernatural woman causes a mountain to erupt and destroy a village.

"People saw Creek Woman as the most beautiful woman in the world, walking through the forest. Hummingbirds floated around her

150: (facing) *Creek Woman* pendant. This supernatural woman resides at the headwaters of salmon creeks and streams. Among the Tsimshian she is sometimes called Fog Woman or Volcano Woman.

151: (left) Creek Woman in Haida stories is sometimes merged with the "grandmother" of the Eagle clans, *Djila'qons*, who was also the beloved wife of Raven in primordial times. The *Djila'qons* stories are similar to those of Volcano Woman. Marcel has carved Creek Woman in argillite with small catlinite flowers and hummingbirds in her flowing hair. Each flower has an abalone centre. The silver bezel surrounding the argillite is filled with a yew wood carving of a humming bird drinking from a flower on the left.

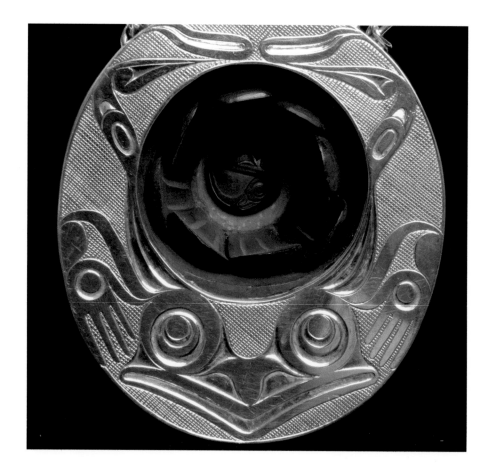

152: (above) The back of the *Creek Woman* pendant is a silver disk engraved with a frog design. The centre of the pendant is hollowed to make it lighter. There Marcel has carved a tiny sleeping hummingbird inside a flower.

153: (upper facing) Marcel has carved a small feast dish in the shape of a bear.

154: (lower facing) Turned upside down, the bear's head has another animal face carved on its lower jaw. Thus, the hidden animal shares the bear's mouth.

head, holding strands of her hair like a veil. Little flowers were nestled in it." Marcel surrounded the argillite figure of Creek Woman with a hummingbird carved in boxwood and set in a silver bezel. The silver back of the pendant is engraved with a frog design, and the argillite has been hollowed out to reveal a baby hummingbird sleeping in a flower. There are tiny hummingbirds carved into her hair.

The pendant epitomizes Marcel's mastery of mixed media, his inspired versatility in artistic themes and techniques, and his quest to excel in innovative vision as a contemporary Haida artist. His interpretations and motivation are firmly grounded in Haida tradition as well as in his own imagination. It's a successful mix. The marketplace has come to his door in Haida Gwaii. For Marcel, success means the joy and excitement of creating art. That is what keeps him going rather than the financial rewards that allow him a certain freedom in his artistic expression:

The hardest thing to do is to take the issue of money out of it and just do art for the art itself. Money is the big bonus at the end if people buy the pieces, but you have to do the art for yourself and for the piece of art itself—not for the almighty dollar. It loses something in translation from your mind to your hand if money gets in the way. It's no good to diminish yourself just to make money.

Argillite suits me so well because I'm very contemporary—out there. I follow traditional rules to a certain point, but after that I just open the doors and let it flow and see where I go from there.

When it comes to argillite, I just let my emotions fly. I may be angry, I may be happy—people feel it and touch it and they see that's the way I was feeling when I did the piece. Some sculptures are smiling, some pieces are about anger and fighting, some pieces are just for having fun. It keeps the naturalness in what I do; it shows how I feel about what I see in my life.

Every day I'm grateful for what I have and what I've achieved. It's a great honour and a privilege to be Haida. I'm in awe of my culture and my people. Everyday I thank the Creator—Salaana—and our spirit ancestors—Kuuniisii.

These days, his passion is divided between his own art and the work he tries to do for his community. A Skidegate elder, Pete Thompson, convinced Marcel that Haida Gwaii badly needed an art school. Once the proposal had been approved and funding was in place, Marcel began to teach. His students were all ages, from the younger kids who studied painting and design, to mid-teens who came to learn to carve masks and handle sharp tools, to adults who consulted him about more advanced techniques. Many are studying Haida dance and song, and making the regalia that go with it. "I tell anyone who wants to learn: 'Respect what I teach and what you are learning.'"

Marcel's belief in passing on knowledge clearly fits his philosophy of building community and keeping a nation alive. He's deeply committed to sharing knowledge, giving back, and raising people's confidence and self-esteem. It's something that he hopes to pass on to his three daughters—Nikita, Alex, and McKenzie Russ-Morrison:

I taught kids who had earned the privilege of attending the art school through keeping their grades up. There was no real pressure to perform in doing art or dance. Art is meant to be fun. Children in this culture can get lost in striving for material things, forgetting their culture; they can get left behind. Part of the deal with the art school was that the parents could come too.

I didn't set parameters or dates that the kids had to do things. I just invited them to come and sit, watch and make their own art. I showed them techniques and how to do their own interpretations. I'd like to take them on field trips to learn how to gather fish, clams and devilfish because the environment is the basis of our art. It's how we get our imaginations going and acknowledge our culture and our home. I believe that you need to learn that—to touch and feel the world—before you can make art.

Marcel's innovative projects, goals and philosophies are still evolving at a whirlwind pace—and yet he finds time to create his own art in argillite, wood, silver, gold, ivory, jade, hardwoods, and sandblasted glass. His vision, ever sharpening, is fundamental to the way he lives, the way he creates. Marcel Russ compares his life to his process of creating art:

The thing I've learned about art is that there's no wrong way of doing it. People will try to say to me, "No, that isn't right!"

"No," I tell them, "You're wrong. It's art. There's no right way or wrong way. Art is art."

A good piece of art is never finished; it's a continually growing thing. You have to remember that you can't get stopped in one place, you have to continually grow or you'll get stagnant. It's fun creating art. I enjoy it—it's my whole life.

155: (facing) *Five-finned Killer Whale and Woman Transforming into an Octopus.* The Eagle lineages of Ninstints (*Sgang Gwaii 'Ilnagaay*) and Chaatl (*T'saahl 'Ilnagaay*) used this supernatural Killer Whale as a crest. Marcel has shown the whale on the back of a woman transforming into an octopus or devilfish. She grasps the whale's pectoral fins in her hands while her legs, transformed into a skirt of tentacles, swirl behind her and envelop the whale's tail. She wears a butterfly necklace across her bare breasts.

JAY SIMEON
Digweegay Tao

As Jay Simeon picks up a chunk of argillite, he says, "I can *feel* what's in there." In a crowded but tidy garage studio filled with fragrant cedar chips, he pauses in his woodcarving as his fingers trace along a slab of stone that has been cut into an elongated rectangle. The motion silences him; he's lost in deep, almost meditative thought. Far away from Haida Gwaii, Jay sits in the middle of a big city, yet even the din of traffic outside seems to fade.

It's a moment in time, touching the raw argillite, but for Jay it may well be 200 years ago in a Haida Gwaii longhouse. He feels near to his ancestral home of Kiusta *(K'yuust'aa)*, close to the master artists of the past, connected to the stories and legends so vital to his artistic sensibilities.

In a career spanning just two decades, Jay has joined the elite of contemporary Northwest Coast artists who have mastered a wide range of media and achieved high acclaim, yet he describes himself as a perpetual student of the art, always learning, always striving to learn.

Life began for Jay in a very different environment. Born in Fort Macleod, Alberta, his childhood was spent with his mother, Lenora Yellow Horn, in the tiny village of Brockett on a Blackfoot reserve in the foothills of the Rockies. He remembers in those early years being fascinated with making art:

My mother told me that one day she thought I was being pretty quiet, so she came to check on me. I was four or five at the time. She found me all alone in my room, colouring pictures in a book. She said I was always pretty intense about doing art. I remember that art was all I wanted to do as a child.

When he was nine, he left Brockett and moved to Vancouver with his father, Eric Simeon, from Old Masset. Jay calls himself "a displaced Haida" who considers his father's village his home.

I guess I just migrated to the coast with my dad. Seems I traded the wind for the rain when we moved from the prairies to the coast. I didn't have to walk around with rocks in my pockets any more; got an umbrella instead. I've been here ever since.

My dad always took an interest in my art. He's the major factor in my art life. He told me that I was Haida and therefore I had to strive to be the best. I always want to make him proud. He died in '93; he was my best friend. He's buried in Masset, but his picture always sits on my desk.

I'll always remember sitting with him and looking at books on Northwest Coast design. I knew right away from his explanations and from what I was seeing that this was a great art form. I was mesmerized by the old pieces, wondering always: "How did they do that?" I knew from that point on I wanted to be a Northwest Coast artist.

Jay's first foray into Northwest Coast art was copying serigraph prints in books. He examined formline design and tried to decipher the principles or rules that he perceived in the way the lines became forms and related to one another. He would look at an ovoid and try to understand why and where it was placed in the two-dimensional designs.

When he was 14, his father introduced him to his "auntie" Sharon Hitchcock, a prominent Haida printmaker, carver, painter and book illustrator. In the 1970s she was one of the few female Haida artists successfully selling her work in galleries. She worked with master carver Bill Reid, designing and drawing the killer whale design on the bow and stern of his now-famous traditional red cedar canoe, *Lootaas* or "Wave Eater". Sharon took a deep interest in the talented youngster, whom she nicknamed Kiusta Boy, and mentored him for several years:

I didn't really understand formline design until I was introduced to my "auntie" Sharon. She lived in Tsawassan and my dad would take me to visit her for a few weeks at a ime. She was deeply involved in the art at that time. I'd just sit with her as she explained the fundamentals of Haida design. After listening to her explain it to me, things started to make sense. I understood how to make a U-form come off an ovoid and how to change the thickness of a formline to suit the image.

She helped me a lot when it came to design. I'd draw or paint something and she'd critique it. We'd do that over and over again. One day, I brought her a piece, and a light bulb just went off in my head—it just clicked—I understood how formline design worked. I'll be forever grateful to my auntie for giving me the opportunity to learn. If it wasn't for Sharon Hitchcock, I wouldn't be where I am today.

Once I could understand the fundamentals, I dove into becoming more educated about Haida art and my heritage. I looked at old designs and understood how far I'd have to go to reach that level. The old artists produced complex images. Understanding how they accomplished that was very humbling to say the least.

Jay had found his passion. The world of books and museums became his classroom as he learned about Haida stories, history and traditions. For a few years he continued to work exclusively in painting and drawing, ever refining his understanding of Northwest Coast design. By the time he was 21, Jay felt he was ready to create in three dimensions. He left Vancouver and moved into the interior of British Columbia. Working with First Nations artist Gary Leon in Williams Lake, he started by carving yellow cedar masks and a small crest pole. "He was my first teacher in sculpture at a time when I wasn't yet confident with carving tools. He gave me the opportunity to express myself. I stayed there a year and finished school." Two years later, having grown in confi-

155

156, 157: Jay Simeon.

dence and experience, Jay moved back to the Vancouver area and he assisted the Squamish band in carving a traditional 40-foot ocean-going canoe.

Jay's quest to become a master artist was fuelled by a deeply held belief that he needed to be "fluent" in every medium used by old and contemporary Northwest Coast artists: paint, wood, silver and gold. Jewellery design—the combination of two-dimensional formlines with three-dimensional forms—intrigued him. He worked with a distant relative, Dwayne Simeon, for six months learning to engrave metals. Following that, Jay continued his enthusiasm for jewellery, studying for a year at Vancouver Community College where he learned repoussé (a relief technique that comes from hammering the metal from the reverse side) and casting techniques. Versatile and innovative jewellery design has become one of Jay's great strengths.

In Vancouver, Jay met emerging argillite carver and art dealer Andrew Williams and shared a studio in the Gastown area of the city. Andrew inspired Jay to add argillite to his repertoire. He first approached the medium by carving mostly flat pieces.

I fell in love with argillite, first of all because it was from home and exclusive to the Haida. I just found a great deal of pleasure in the stone—it's wonderful to hold in your hands: smooth, cool and workable. I found with argillite my ideas could go from my heart to my head and out my fingertips. The ideas just seemed to flow faster than when I was working in wood or metals.

When I was just starting out in argillite, carving poles and medallions in the Gastown studio, I began to get a little bit of an ego. Then one day Christian White popped in and nonchalantly put a $50,000 argillite box on my bench. I dropped my tools and dropped my jaw. I was completely blown away by this miniature chief's chest. The corners of the box rested on frogs; the sides were fully sculptural. His inlays were immaculate. I think that's when I heard the ancestors telling me, "You're not that good." It sure put me in my place.

The Gastown studio expanded when Marcel Russ came to Vancouver and was invited to join Andrew and Jay. Marcel recalls Jay clearly: "He was pretty quiet, shy almost. He wouldn't really even look at me or talk to me for a few months." Eventually, Jay connected with Marcel, and rapidly began to learn new ideas about sculpting stone from the more experienced argillite carver. "Marcel taught me a lot about how far you can push the medium," he says. Marcel in turn was impressed by Jay's sheer drive to learn and his attention to fine detail as he quickly absorbed Marcel's instruction. Working and learning side-by-side, they developed a deep friendship and shared ideas about technique, tools, materials and where they wanted to take their art.

156

158: (above) Trained in jewellery-making, Jay often surrounds his wearable argillite sculptures with silver bezels to create pendants. This elaborate pendant is Volcano Woman, who weeps for her frog children who were thoughtlessly thrown into the fire by hunters. Exacting revenge, she causes a volcanic eruption that smothers the hunters' village. In this pendant, her tears are the forelegs of a frog under her chin. She shares power with the frog through shared tongues.

159: (left facing) Jay's first argillite sculpture, *Beaver's Lake,* illustrates the story of Beaver who, according to Tsimshian legend, dammed a stream to swim in and was transformed into a supernatural Beaver. In the beginning of time, the voracious Raven stole Beaver's lake and the salmon in it. As he flew away with his prize, Eagle chased him and he dropped some of the lake and some of the salmon to the earth, creating the lakes and salmon streams of the Northwest Coast.

160: (right facing) Haida Eagle clans use the Beaver as a crest which they received from the children of Property Making A Noise, who survived the volcanic eruption caused by *Djila'qons* in revenge for hunters killing her frog children. Visually, the beavers are portrayed with large incisors, a gnawing stick, and a crosshatched tail with a face where the tail joins the body.

Marcel really helped me at that time by pushing me into doing three-dimen-sional sculpture. I was kinda timid at that time. He wanted me to leave the flat or panel style behind and do more sculptural pieces. He encouraged me to carve the piece first in my mind. He said then when it came to actually carving the piece, it would almost be an afterthought. Easier said than done, but I did learn that from him.

With my training in jewellery, I tended to work out everything on paper. With argillite, the real work is done in the mind; you have to figure out where you're going and choose the right piece. I still first draw what I'm going to create—but I do that less with argillite.

When I draw an image for an argillite piece, it always changes when I go from the paper to the stone. Argillite sculpture evolves; the stone has a life of its own and it knows what it wants to be. You're just there to chip away the excess and let the image out.

Jay's first major sculpture, called *Beaver's Lake*, depicts an episode in primordial times when a large supernatural Beaver controlled a huge lake filled with salmon. In the Haida story, Raven steals that lake. Jay's

158

161: (above left) Jay's love of combining silver and argillite has been inspired by his teacher, the noted Haida artist Sharon Hitchcock. Jay's small argillite bentwood box is a replica of a type made from a single wooden plank that was grooved or kerfed in three places, steamed, bent and then stitched or pegged to form a box or bowl. The sides of the box were fitted into a grooved base and similarly fastened. A solid thick plank with flaring sides comprised the box's lid.

162: (above right) Jay's box is incised with a formline design. Human and Killer Whale forms are compressed to tell the Nanasimgat story of the man who rescues his kidnapped wife from a supernatural orca. On a wooden box, these designs would have been painted; here they are incised and carved in low relief.

163: (right) The lid of Jay's argillite box has the image of Raven with outstretched wings and mighty talons. Argillite artists, both in the past and present, frequently employ the rope-like border that Jay has used to define the edge of the box lid.

164: (facing) Jay and one of his teachers, Marcel Russ, carved side-by-side when he created this argillite crest pole. The top figure is a female shaman holding round rattles. Two watchmen or *skil* flank her. Eagle is the dominant figure on the base of the pole.

sculpture, however, illustrates the period before Raven arrives. The beaver is depicted sitting on his haunches. He has large ivory incisors and holds a gnawing stick in his paws; three leaping salmon surround his scaly tail. The human face in Beaver's elaborately carved tail is the clue that this is a giant supernatural Beaver.

I'd call that my break-through sculpture. It's probably the first fully dimensional argillite piece I attempted. Even to this day I get a lot of ribbing from Andrew and Marcel because when I started to carve, it was a 20- to 25-pound chunk of argillite. I just worked and worked on that thing. The finished sculpture is only about five inches tall and five inches wide at the base. When I was done, the guys just laughed at me and said, "You could've made three sculptures out of that chunk. You sure waste a lot of slate." I just brush them off—which I have to do pretty much every time I see them these days— and say, "Well, it was my chunk of argillite!"

In a box with a Raven design on the lid, Jay combines argillite and silver, an idea that he appreciates in works by Sharon Hitchcock and Bill Reid. With attention to fine detail, he replicates on the sides of the silver lid the adze blade marks that are often found on the large cedar chief's boxes.

Jay completed an argillite crest pole in the Gastown studio while sitting at the desk next to Marcel Russ. He considers it as perhaps the best example of his maturing style. "In it, I had the opportunity to use all of Marcel's techniques on one piece. I thought it was a big accomplishment. Marcel was doing a pole at the same time, next to me." The top of Jay's pole depicts a female shaman with circular rattles. She is flanked by two *skils* or watchmen. Below the shaman is Beaver, then Eagle with Frogs in his ears, holding on to a salmon and exchanging tongues with another frog. The complexity, detail and fineness of inlay are a tribute to how well Jay learned from Marcel.

Jay credits many Haida and non-Haida Northwest Coast artists with teaching and inspiring him. After Marcel Russ and Sharon Hitchcock, his principle teachers and sources of inspiration have been Fred Davis, Rick Atkins, Christian White, Don Yeomans, Philip Gray, Cory Bullpit, Gerry Marks, Reggie Davidson, Corey Moraes, his uncles George and John Yeltatzie, and Gary Minaker Russ.

Yeah, especially Gary. Wow. I think I'm going to have to lock him out of Vancouver. Next time he plans to visit from the island I'm going put posters on the ferry that say not to let him come across. He's draining the art economy with all that good work of his!

The reality is, all these people have had an impact on me. They're all stars. If I could put all these artists on trading cards, you know, like the ones you get for basketball players, I'd collect them all from their rookie cards right up to their pro cards. And I wouldn't ever trade them.

That's what keeps me going. Learning, talking with other artists who are so good. There's so much room to grow, and when I do that it just lights a fire under me. It means I have to reach, stretch, take risks—and that takes courage. It's easy to play it safe, especially when you've done something that is a commercial success. The gallery may want you to repeat the same thing. But for me, I try to do something new. I'm always learning, and there's so much to learn.

Though he has strong connections to his combined Blackfoot and Haida heritage, Jay's art is all Haida. He is a proud member of the Kaawaas branch of the *Sdast'a.aas* Eagle clan that originated in Kiusta, an ancient village site located on the northwestern tip of Haida Gwaii, north of Old Masset. His family crests include Eagle, Killer Whale, Cormorant, Frog, Beaver, Flicker and Raven. His Haida name is *Digweegay Tao,* "Strength of the Copper", given to him by Sharon Hitchcock and his late naanii, Flossie Yeltatzie.

Being Haida means a lot to me. The Haida have so much history and tradition. I was always intrigued by the old stories of the Haida roaming all over the Pacific. They were some bad dudes in those days—raiding and taking slaves. More than that, though, they've been carving masterpieces for over 200 years, and the world acknowledges that. I work hard in my life and art to maintain the standard that the old timers laid down for us. I've been mesmerized by their old pieces for as long as I can remember.

If you want to be as good as they were, I tell people, you have to work at it every day. It's like striving to be Michael Jordan. This guy's incredible but he works at it all the time. It's the same thing in my art. I go back and look at the old pieces and learn something new every time. Sometimes I don't go back that far. I definitely look at the work Bill Reid and Robert Davidson have done and get really inspired. The excellence in their works teaches me.

His advice for young artists is to study and learn. "I'm more than happy to help," he says. "A lot of people helped me. But, just look at the Internet and in the galleries. There are a lot of new people doing fantastic stuff." He already considers the future bright for young Northwest Coast artists coming behind him and is eager to watch their successes.

Like Darrell White. He's so good and he just came out of the blue. Some of his pieces are just unbelievable: a real testament to this artist, his determination and his innovation. Like using gold tongues on his argillite figures. That's crazy; some of the things he's coming up with blow me away.

I have a tendency to over-analyze what I'm doing; I can be a bit of a perfectionist, which is not as good as just going for it. If you try to be perfect, you'll soon find that when you look at other artists' stuff, there's always someone better than you, someone more proficient in a certain technique or medium. That drives me nuts—especially when you're born Haida. You're supposed to be good!

It all goes back to the old timers and the high standards that they set in their art. It's exciting to see a new generation of artists study, listen and progress in their art. We're all working together, all pushing each other forward—and that's fantastic for the future of Haida art and all Northwest Coast art. The future for us is so bright!

As accomplished and successful as he is, Jay Simeon considers himself a life-long student of Northwest Coast art. With optimism, humility and a good measure of humour, Jay relishes each new project, each new challenge to present to the world something of himself and what it means to be Haida.

161

165: (upper facing) Jay's *Bear Feast Bowl* is an argillite replica of northern Northwest Coast feast dishes that were also made in the same way as kerfed or bentwood boxes. The northern bowls always had the undulating rim, carved high on the ends and low on the sides, that Jay has reproduced in stone. Like the wooden object, Jay has made one end highly three-dimensional by sculpting the head and paws of a bear.

166: (lower facing) The rims of traditional bentwood feast bowls were inlaid with operculum. Jay substituted opals that resembled the much larger opercula.

DARRELL WHITE
K̲ats'-stl'iinaa

If Darrell White had a middle name, it would probably be the Haida equivalent of "precision", for that is exactly what comes from his hands when he creates argillite sculpture. Everything is precise about this man. His studio occupies a small but extremely organized space. Uniformly sized bins of inlay materials, neatly sorted, rest under a shelf containing four open boxes of drill sets. The drill bits gleam in contrast to the dull dark gray of the raw blocks of argillite on the next shelf. Books, clippings and photographs depicting Northwest Coast art and history fill the walls and shelves behind his workstation. For a place where argillite is carved, there is a remarkable lack of the usual black dust. There is nothing out of place; the space projects the orderly thoughtfulness of an artist who prides himself on exactness and clean design.

Darrell is master of creating monumental argillite sculptures that are miniature in size. He delights in innovation and creating the unexpected. In his hands a tiny rattle is fashioned so that Raven holds a clamshell under his chin, nestled against his body. The bottom of the shell, next to the handle, has opened to reveal three startled faces of the first men to emerge into the world. Precisely, Darrel fits a rim of thin gold wire around the incised edge of the clamshell above their heads and plans how he will invisibly secure it to the stone. He smiles, lifts the little rattle between forefinger and thumb, gives a quick shake. The rattle vibrates with the trade beads he has already sealed within its hollowed interior. He laughs.

162

167: (right) Darrell fits the rim of an argillite clamshell with 18k gold wire on the *Raven and the First Men* rattle pendant.

168: (upper facing) Darrell White.

169: (left facing) The completed *Raven and the First Men* rattle pendant is miniature in size but monumental in scale. Viewed from the back, Darrell has paid particular attention to the details of the inlaid wings and tail feathers. Despite its small size, it is an accurate interpretation of Haida rattles; moreover, it is a functional rattle, with trade beads sealed in its hollow interior.

170: (right facing) From the front, Raven cradles his treasure, a clamshe ll containing the First Men, against his breast. The artist has intricately inlaid the argillite shell with abalone, rimmed it with gold wire, and also wrapped the handle with gold.

Peers, gallery owners, and clients alike express astonishment when they first view Darrell's artworks; they are even more amazed to learn that this artist burst onto the Northwest Coast art scene a relatively short time ago as an apparently fully mature sculptor. Darrell carved his first piece of argillite in 1999 at age 39 and by the beginning of this century was selling in high-end galleries, his work fetching top dollar. His fast-tracking new career in art bypassed many of the usual obligatory stops a lot of Northwest Coast artists have taken on their way to the top. "I really didn't know any better," he says almost apologetically, "I just took my first work right into the best galleries, told them what I wanted, and they bought it outright. I guess I sort of skipped a few steps, but it's worked well for me so far."

Born in Queen Charlotte City on Haida Gwaii, Darrell, his sister April and brother Geoffrey moved to the interior of British Columbia in early 1966 with mother Linda, eventually settling in Powell River. Darrell went to school in that community, earned his ticket as a welder in Vancouver, and developed a career as a contractor to the pulp and paper, forestry, fishing, and mining industries. His children, Alanna, Tanya, and Mitchell, were born while he lived in Powell River. Trips home to Haida Gwaii were infrequent; Darrell didn't maintain the same closeness to his family and his cultural heritage that his sister did— something that would change later in his life.

Some serious art and artists run in Darrell's family. His great great grandfather was the renowned Haida artist Charles Edenshaw. His cousins Jim Hart and Christian White have well-established careers as artists and cultural leaders. His sister April White is well known as an innovative and excellent painter, printmaker and watercolourist. Although Darrell appreciated their work and greatly admired traditional Haida art, he put family life and career before his desire to do the art himself.

I was pretty much a dabbler in Haida art until 2002. I'd started a red cedar bowl in 1989, but never finished it. I did my first piece of argillite in 1999 and the following year started some argillite pendants and medallions. They're pretty rough. When I look at them now, I laugh. I had no training, lots of books to look at, but not a lot of time to practise art. Then in 2002, I made a decision that I needed a change—I call this my "crisis year"—because I knew I wanted to carve and become a professional artist, but I had to weigh that against leaving a steady job. This wasn't just an impulse; it's almost as if there was a force that wanted me to be an artist. An unstoppable force.

With courage and a meagre income as a buffer, Darrell found himself plunging into deep water. He moved out of Powell River and set up a studio. From 2002–2003 he received a sponsorship from Community Futures and through their program consulted an accountant and developed a business plan that supported his vision.

That first year in the program I carved a cedar pole and a frontlet—mostly on my own brain power. Up to that time I hadn't studied the art a lot, and I wasn't working with any other native artists. The pole and frontlet were done with enough skill that they sold and paid the rent, but most of all I was able to make the transition from a regular income into being a full-time carver.

The big shift in his artistic career came when he accepted an invitation from his cousin Christian White to come to Old Masset in the winter of 2002.

For about 10 days, I went to work with him. He said to me, "Design something and I'll help you." So I laid out a small panel pipe on paper. I began carving and sometimes stayed up all night working on it. Christian showed me step-by-step how to carve it, from roughing it out to finishing it. I'd carve for a couple of hours, get stuck—just come to a screeching halt. Then he'd take it, carve a little as he talked to me, and hand it back. I'd be off again until I had to stop again, and we'd do the same thing. He showed me how to do inlays, how he used catlinite—everything I needed to know about carving argillite sculpture.

Finally, I returned to my studio and finished a yellow cedar model pole, the argillite pipe I'd started in Haida Gwaii, and then I carved a frontlet

*in argillite. I was amazed when the argillite sold right away to a Florida
collector through a Vancouver gallery. It was a time of high stress—the kids
were living with me by then—but I kept going.*

With a voracious appetite that rivalled the mythical Raven, Darrell
began studying the work of the old Haida masters—Charles Edenshaw
and Charles's uncle Albert Edward Edenshaw, to name two—as well as
the more recent masters such as Bill Reid, his cousins Jim and Christian,
and Robert Davidson.

*I found my life somewhat paralleled Bill Reid's, who also began studying and
learning about his Haida heritage later in life. Bill called it "becoming Haida"
and I guess I felt that same kind of drive to catch up with my birth culture.
I've been away most of my life, so it's something that I'm learning. Every
time I meet Haida relatives I'm reacquainting myself with the culture. Up to
recently, I've been isolated from my heritage, but I'm getting it back. I never
really knew my dad until I was 39, but now he's a big part of my life. He
teaches me a lot and I listen to him speaking Haida. You might say I'm a bit of
a work in progress.*

*I study the old timers. I don't claim to have a complete understanding
of formline design—I'm learning it as I go. I look at old work, like Charles
Edenshaw's boxes, and see how he did them; think about it too. Many artists
have that traditional nephew-uncle relationship where this knowledge is
passed from one generation to the other over the years. I don't have that kind
of luxury. I find my teachers in the old works. I borrow from them; that's how
I learn.*

165

Part of "becoming Haida" meant remembering his early life on Haida
Gwaii. In 1998 Darrell attended an event surrounding the Edenshaw
exhibition at the UBC Museum of Anthropology, which reinforced his
interest in Haida art. Through Jim Hart he reconnected with his dad,
Brian White. This gave greater impetus to make visits to his father's
village of Old Masset, where he attended potlatches and cultural events.
A member of the *Yahgu 'laanaas* Raven clan that originated in the
ancient village of Dadens *(Daa.adans)*, Darrell received his first Haida
name as an adult in 1999 at the memorial potlatch for Morris White.
"Auntie Joan [Hart] and great auntie Lavina [White] called me *Kats'-
stl'iinaa,* or 'Prickly-hair like a sea urchin.'"

*They chuckled, even chortled in obvious joy over their unique choice, claiming
maybe one day we'll give you a more serious name. At the time my hair
was short and thick and would stand straight up. Now it's long, thick, and
hangs from the weight, but talking to Aunty Joan recently, she still smiles and
chuckles, "You have a good name." I can't help but smile and laugh too.*

The first trip he made to Slatechuck Mountain to collect argillite
was with his cousin Christian in 2002. The labour-intensive experience

imprinted Darrell with a greater appreciation for the uniqueness and value of his chosen medium:

That first year I worked with Christian we decided to go to the mountain for slate. That's a five-kilometre hike or slightly less from the beach. Every trip is different; it's always soggy and sometimes it can be treacherous, especially on the heavily laden return trip. With a missed step, under a heavy load the potential for sprains, strains and injury is high.

That winter day the trail was misty and there was fog among the huge cedars. Christian hadn't been to the mountain for years. It was a very spiritual experience for both of us—invigorating and physically draining all at once. He sang a thank-you song that echoed on the trail. It was my first time, so I thought I'd pack out 100 pounds; lost my footing right away.

It is not surprising that one of Darrell's first argillite sculptures, completed in 2003, was called *Between Worlds* and depicts a transformational moment that parallels the transformations going on in his own life at the time. The sculpture resembles a soul catcher used by shamans in healing rituals. Traditionally carved from bone, the soul catcher has open-mouthed heads at either end and often a human face between the heads. The shaman would recover the "lost" soul of a sick person, seal it inside the hollow soul catcher with shredded cedar bark, and then reinsert the soul back into the patient's body to restore health and well-being.

In *Between Worlds*, Darrell fashioned his own argillite soul catcher as a double-headed killer whale with a shaman draped over the middle of their conjoined backs. The shaman wears an octopus headdress. Octopus, or devilfish, is frequently a spirit helper for shamans and is one of Darrell's crests. The base of the soul catcher depicts a high-ranking woman with a labret dressed in a ceremonial blanket and dancing apron. Perhaps through this sculpture Darrell had restored some of his own Haida soul.

Darrel continued to visit Haida collections in museums, travel around Haida Gwaii, and read books on Northwest Coast art, "especially the original sources from people like John Swanton and James Swan, who wrote down Haida stories." He began making connections between what he read and what he saw in archival photographs and in museum collections. These experiences were rapidly amalgamated with his Haida Gwaii experiences and translated into his personal artistic vision. It wasn't long before Darrell defined his own style:

I wanted to make my sculptures wearable art so I turned many of them into pendants. I got the idea of using gold with argillite almost right away. I'd always liked the inlays Northwest Coast artists used in their work, and for me it was a natural to adapt some of the basic skills I'd learned in fabricating custom pieces for industry to these much smaller objects. I knew how to cold hammer metal and I had the knowledge for fashioning basic tools to do this on a smaller scale.

The first year, I made all the beaver teeth on my sculptures in gold. Then I put gold tongues on the bear, dogfish and salmon-trout heads on a lidded argillite box. The gold tongues are neat and domed. Now every tongue on my work seems to be gold or it doesn't look right to me. Lately, I've been making the nostrils on Thunderbirds gold as well.

Having quickly reached a high level of competence and inspiration as a sculptor, Darrell works full time in his studio creating masterpieces in argillite. He's happy working small: "I don't have to make it big to make it have impact," he says confidently. "None of my works are really big, they just seem larger than they are because I give them a jewel-like quality." He laughs, unwilling to take himself too seriously, "and of course, some people like sparkly things!"

Darrell's process involves as much precision in thinking about what he is going to carve as the sculpting techniques he employs:

I don't draw what I'm going to carve first. I can run it over in my mind for several months or so. I have to think about what I'm going to do. Sometimes the stone makes the decision, but mostly it's me thinking ahead and envi-

167

171: (facing) *Between Worlds* is Darrell's interpretation of a shaman's soul catcher. The shaman appears to have octopus tentacles coming from his head, symbolizing his own supernatural helper. The shaman clasps the dorsal fins of two opposing killer whales. Note how Darrell carefully planned two of the tentacles to overlap the catlinite ovoids of the orcas' pectoral fins. With characteristic precision and attention to fine detail the artist has fashioned mastodon ivory teeth in the mouths of the killer whales and on the bear tooth necklace of the shaman.

172: (above) Darrell's *Killer Whale Clan* pendant is an example of wearable art. A human figure grasps the orca's bifurcated tail in his hands and peers through the cleft in the tail. To keep the design field compact, Darrel has split the whale's dorsal fin and spread it on either side of the body—a well-known Northwest Coast artistic convention to rearrange parts of an image to fit a given field. Shown here almost twice its actual size, this sculpture is indeed monumental.

173, 174: (facing) A masterpiece of carving and inlay, Darrell's argillite kerfed chief's box has identical bear heads on the short sides. Bear on one of the long sides and Shark on the other have protruding tongues finished in 18k gold.

175: (left) On the box lid, the artist has carved Berry Picker Woman in the Moon, one of his own crests. Flawlessly inlaid with abalone shell, a corona gleams around her face that is carved in high relief on top of the box. Gold inlays are used for the face painting that, along with the large labret in her lower lip, indicate her high rank and wealth.

176: (below) A mere 3.5 cm tall, Darrell's *Raven and Clam Shell Panel Pipe* is unexpected and innovative, not only for the lavish gold, catlinite and abalone inlays, but also for the round shape of the pipe. Compact and jewel-like, the pipe is a new interpretation of an ancient theme: Raven discovering the First Men in a clamshell. He envelops his treasure with wings, claws and tail as he exchanges tongues with one of the emerging humans. The tongue is gold – could this be symbolic of the soothing song Raven sings to his foundlings as told in some Haida stories?

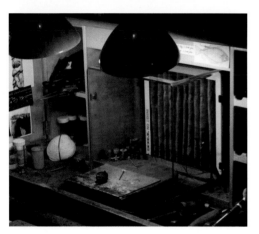

177-179: Darrell's meticulous process begins with the use of templates to plan his inlays (top). Carefully he removes the outer surface of the abalone shell to find the best colour patterns (centre). His workstation (bottom), which he designed himself, is portable and contains a powerful dust filter to keep the black argillite dust under control.

180-182: (facing) Darrell's *Legends of the Haida Crest Pole* is as intricate as it is exquisitely inlaid. Crowned by Eagle with his sharply downturned beak and holding a salmon in his talons, the pole's figures are almost organically intertwined. Below Eagle, Bear Mother holds her two cubs and exchanges golden tongues with Frog. The large figure below her is the supernatural Killer Whale who has kidnapped Gunarhnesemgyet's wife. The husband is shown pushing himself through the orca's blowhole (detail right). Darrell has hollowed the reverse of the pole and revealed the backside of Gunarh.

sioning what I'm going to do. I'll pencil the image on the stone, and I won't carve anything on it until I'm happy with it. My general guideline is to make a series of decisions: will it be a Raven or an Eagle crest? How will the figures be related? That means I've figured out where all the images will go, where I want the inlays to be, and how everything will be entwined together.

There are some techniques I use from my past training. I make a lot of measurements, and I work from a centreline so that when the design's all laid out it's square, balanced and symmetrical.

Most carving, he claims, can be done with no more than a half dozen basic hand tools, a few files, and some small handsaws:

My scribers are taken directly from my welding days. Christian made my first two main argillite carving tools, which I still use today. From these I have added different sizes, but the same basic shape, and I have also made different shapes and sizes as needed. I've made some tools out of chain saw files; each end is a different shape—a blade or a gouge. I use some of the same tools as I did earlier in my life: knives and gravers, squares, callipers and compasses. They're just smaller.

I try to save power tools for initial shaping and hollowing, so I can have more time for the important stuff. They do create more of a mess, however, so by hand is best for the most part. They are also good for shaping and polishing the inlays, which can be quite hard.

Darrell's inlay work is characterized by meticulous precision. His 18k gold pieces are fashioned on a tiny yew wood anvil with a jeweller's hammer and a tiny chain saw file. Various templates control the exact shape of catlinite, abalone, or mastodon ivory inlays so that he can shape them with the same precision that he would use to plan a bolt pattern on a piece of steel. "There's no guess work that way," he says. His gold wire applications are wrapped, tapped flat by a hammer, or cut by hand. When the argillite is finished, he may soften some corners with 2000 grit sandpaper, but he uses it sparingly. Mostly Darrell prefers tool finishing. "I liked the look of Christian's finishing; the tool finish shows the rhythm of the artist working."

For his own workspace, Darrell designed a compact "oyster shell" wooden box that opens to reveal two small storage cupboards flanking a large air filter intake—hence the lack of argillite dust. "I wanted my workbench to be truly portable," he says, "and when I'm working with grinding abalone or carving argillite and the dust they generate, I don't want to breathe it in." For this argillite artist, at least, there's no "breathing stone."

When it comes to carving, Darrell's favourites are Bear and Raven. He also depicts other images from his own crests: Two-finned Killer-Whale, Grizzly, Shark or Dogfish, Berry Picker in the Moon, and Devilfish or Octopus. Darrell's sculptures often contain a surprise or an interesting hook to intrigue his viewers. On one pole, a man's face peering through a killer whale's blowhole is completed by showing the human's bare backside on the back of the pole, leaving little to the imagination about the person's gender. In an inspired round pipe depicting Raven opening a clamshell from which two men are emerging, the smoker—if this pipe could be smoked—would place his or her lips on the exquisite red catlinite lips of a human supporting the shell. Darrell's sharp humour is not to be missed.

He's fond of providing the viewer with images that are good to think as well as good to see. His repertoire of argillite subjects is far-reaching and always a challenge to create. They are challenges that Darrell enjoys because they demand a combination of thought and skill. Each finished argillite sculpture or pendant demands time to appreciate fully not only for the design and form, but the technical and cultural ideas that have brought it into being. He has many ideas just waiting to become reality, ready to be communicated.

There's a lot yet to do, though, lots to think about. I work exclusively in argillite now. Argillite has always been a small, specific market with only a handful of masters at any given time—which has been true throughout history. Argillite is exclusive to Haida artists and to Haida Gwaii, which suits me just fine.

Meticulousness, elegance, understanding, innovation and humour. These are hallmarks of a master argillite sculptor. Darrell's achievements in the few short years since shifting careers from welder to carver are nothing short of astounding. We shouldn't really be surprised. It's all in the art of fabrication—of bringing together excellence and insight into Haida visual thought—and Darrell White does all that with precision.

LIONEL SAMUELS

183: Alice Williamsen and Lionel Samuels.

184: (facing) A supernatural raven-finned killer whale is depicted leaping out of the ocean waves. Even before he begins carving, Lionel finds images such as this inside a chunk of argillite.

Listening to argillite artist Lionel Samuels is either like holding a tornado by the tail or shaking hands with a fist. Either way, he's a bundle of energy, fully in control of the conversation and moving fast. His unbridled zeal for life is unmistakable as he takes great delight in sharing his story. Like so many other Haida of his generation, Lionel's biography is filled with tragedy and triumphs. In the telling, his personal narrative is sprinkled with jokes and teasing: Haida humour at its best. An artist who is passionate about his life-long work in argillite and about being Haida, Lionel communicates eloquently in words and in stone. Purposefully, he strives to convey powerful ideas about his Haida heritage: the people of Haida Gwaii, their lands and nation, their stories and arts, and their rich cultural history.

Like most Haida, Lionel can trace his family history back for several centuries; it's a connection that he prizes. His most distinguished 18th century ancestor was Connehaw or Gunya *(Gannyaa)*, the powerful chief of Kiusta, Lionel's ancestral home. Gunya's wife, called "Madam Gunya" by the English traders, was well known by early ship captains for her astuteness in bartering for sea otter pelts with the first Euro-American seamen to visit Haida Gwaii. Family stories claim she was one of the first Haida to market argillite sculptures to European and British sailors. This wealthy and prestigious family is often cited in historic ships' journals that record the first Euro-American maritime visits to Haida Gwaii.

Since that time and through the generations, many high-ranking Haida men have held the name Gunya. (Wright, 2001:345). According to Lionel's family, when the descendents of Gunya left Kiusta, they moved to Alaska and to Skidegate near Slatechuck Creek. One of those descendents, George Young, also called George Gunya (1864–1924), was described by the anthropologist Marius Barbeau as owning the argillite quarry and being a carver of scrimshaw and argillite flutes. (Barbeau, 1957:4–9). George Gunya was the uncle of Lionel's great grandfather Andrew Brown or *Owt'iwans*, who was given the title "Captain" because he was the first boat builder to construct a motorized fishing vessel in Haida Gwaii. Today, however, Captain Brown is best known as a prolific artist who carved in wood and argillite. Lionel especially treasures this man in his distinguished lineage.

Owt'iwans' first daughter, Eliza Abrahams, was a weaver of fine cedar bark hats. She was also the last woman in the village to wear a labret, an elaborately carved disk of stone, shell or bone inserted into a piercing beneath the lower lip. As a woman's social rank and wealth increased, her labret increased in size. "When she became aged, she no longer wore it and her lower lip drooped and sagged, because the labret had been so large. You can see this in her photographs," says Lionel. Eliza's daughter was Lillian Abrahams, who married Ruben Samuels. One of their children was Gladys, Lionel's mother. According to Haida matrilineal tradition, Lionel Dexter Samuels was born into the *Yahgu 'laanaas* Raven clan in Queen Charlotte City in 1963.

Lionel's naanii Lillian and tsinii Ruben were responsible for caring for 13 children, including their grandchildren from their own deceased children. After Gladys went to live in Prince Rupert, Lionel grew up with his grandparents in a very crowded house. He was one of the youngest and cried a lot, so he quickly earned the nickname *Chuka'nuung* or "cry baby". Lionel remembers tsinii Ruben, who was a logger and fisherman, telling him, "Never stand with your hands in your pockets lest you be thought of as lazy. When you see a native with his hand out, it is to collect rent, not to beg."

Some of Lionel's early and fondest memories are of living in Old Masset. He remembers "running around naked," hunting baby sharks, making rafts, catching baby deer, and strawberry-picking with his uncle Johnny. It was also the time that he began visiting the home of Flossie Yeltatzie to watch her sons carve argillite:

I must have been about seven or eight years old at the time. I'd just go there and watch all the Yeltatzie boys, especially Terry, John and George. Sharon Hitchcock and Fred Davis were there too, carving. After auntie Flossie moved out, everyone left. Then after five or six years, George moved back into the house. Around 1976, I started hanging out at that same place again, only this time I wasn't just watching. I started learning the basics of carving argillite. Harold Yeltatzie, Claude Davidson, and George Yeltatzie were carving together there. I was in my early teens.

173

At the time I looked at tsinii Brown's work a lot. His sculptures were so different from everyone else's. He carved these big birds with huge spread wings. I was really inspired by him and his work. I decided my first argillite pieces would be two Eagle sculptures like his. I sold them to the chief counsellor at the time. He said he usually didn't buy argillite, but that these were something special. I got $500 apiece for them, which was a lot of money in those days, especially for a young kid. It was then that I started to think I should try to make my living that way.

One day I was sitting in a house that my mother gave me. I was just working at a desk on an argillite piece when George Yeltatzie came over. He looked at what I'd done and started to cry. He said, "That looks just like Owt'iwans' carving. I used to carve with Owt'iwans." That was the day I made the decision to become a professional artist.

In his mid-teens, Lionel apprenticed with Claude Davidson and joined Claude and Sarah's *K'a.adsnee* (Shark House) Dancers. After taking a five-month course in tool making and carving from Claude, he was hired to carve wooden masks for the dancers. "I did Raven, Frog, and Eagle masks. Some of them are still being used today." Sarah recalls that young Lionel was "just delightful and always so cheeky." Lionel

danced with the group, and carved many things for the Haida troupe that performed at Expo 86 in Vancouver. He also began carving with Beau Dick and Ed Russ "behind a shack in front of Claude's house, near the ball field." They were good days, productive and filled with artistic growth.

Tragedy soon struck deeply in Lionel's young life. First tsinii Ruben died, and within a few months his naanii Lillian died as well. Many of the kids in their care, except those belonging to Gladys and Rosseta, were dispersed over a period of time to Vancouver and Victoria. Soon after, Gladys, at age 33, died of a brain aneurism. It was a defining moment in Lionel's life, one that brought negative consequences for years to come:

When I was 17, my mother died in my arms. From that I developed what today we know as post-traumatic stress disorder. My brothers and my sister were put into foster care. All that contributed to me becoming an alcoholic and a drug addict. That's why I'm a little vague on dates and stuff. George Yeltatzie kept me calm after she died; he kept me carving. I was on my own. I was carving, but I also took up drinking.

My drinking caught up to me. I was furious at the village bootlegger for what happened in my family, so I beat him severely, and of course, stole all his booze and drank it. I was charged with assault and the judge gave me a choice: three months in jail or go to a recovery house in Victoria. It was my "government holiday". That was my way out of Masset and I took it.

Lionel was 18 when he was sent to Victoria. He continued making argillite art the entire time he was on probation. When he finished his sentence, he slept under the Johnson Street Bridge and supported himself selling carvings. He went to the Royal British Columbia Museum and saw George Yeltatzie's work in the gift shop; soon he was selling his own work there. In 1985 a new opportunity opened for him:

When I was at the museum I saw a guy repairing some of their argillite collection. He was doing it all wrong—trying to fill up scratches with shoe polish and stuff. I suggested some changes and before I knew it I got a summer job repairing the broken argillite. I got to hold all their old argillite pieces and work with them. One day I picked up an argillite flute and just played it. I'd never played a flute before in my life. I soon found out it was carved by a guy named George Gunya. Of course, I knew that he was related to me.

In Victoria, the museum gift shop and a gallery continued to buy Lionel's argillite sculptures for the next five or six years. During that time, he decided not to return to Haida Gwaii and to stay in Victoria. He kept company with prominent Kwakwaka'wakw artists, Tony Hunt, Jr. and Tony Hunt, Sr. and carved alongside them. Having to travel regularly to Vancouver to sell his argillite sculpture through Hill's Native Art

185: (above) Lionel uses fine chisels to carve details into his argillite sculptures.

186: (upper facing) *Raven Stealing the Light Dancer.* Viewed from one side, this sculpture illustrates a dancer. The man wears a Raven headdress and dancing apron and carries two rattles. Raven on the headdress has a round ball in his beak representing the sun, which he stole from his grandfather in the beginning of time.

187: (lower facing) From the other side, Lionel has carved a two-dimensional Raven on the dancer's blanket. Employing the principle of split-representation in formline design, Lionel has figuratively split the image of Raven's head down the middle and splayed each half in profile above its body and tail feathers to fill the entire surface of the blanket. From this view, with the feathers of the headdress hiding the dancer's human form, it's easy to believe the supernatural Raven himself is being portrayed.

Gallery, Lionel moved to that city to live with his "brother" Woodrow Samuels.

Sobriety soon eluded Lionel. He thought travelling might bring a different life, maybe even a cure for his addictions. The whole time he travelled, he was making small argillite sculptures:

I decided to travel back east. So one March I headed over the Rockies to Calgary. It was so cold I came right back to Vancouver and stayed there until the following June. Then I started out again across Canada. I was hitchhiking. Only natives and rich people seemed to pick me up, but I made it to Ottawa. I sat outside the museum and sold argillite pendants to people going into the museum. Eventually I started selling my argillite in that gift shop for a while.

From Ottawa, I made enough money to go to New York and then down to Washington, D.C. where I got a job working in a booth in their gift shop carving argillite. It wasn't a paying job. I only made money when someone bought an argillite piece from me. The Smithsonian bought one of my sculptures for their collection. I was sober for a few months, and then I made it back to Vancouver.

In Vancouver, I was hired by a gallery to basically guard the store. I carved small sculptures in the window and the owner would sell them to her clients in the States—I think she got a lot more money for them than I ever saw. She tried to keep other dealers and clients from meeting me; I only found that out later.

Lionel decided he wanted to create large sculptures and escape what seemed to him to be an exploitative curio market. His first big piece was a large argillite Frog bowl that he sold to a major Vancouver art gallery. He concentrated on making large sculptures, sometimes carving on the beach at English Bay, and soon he was not only selling to Canadian galleries and clients, but also attracting buyers in the United States, some of them in the movie industry.

In 1987, Lionel was invited by Chief Skidegate and Chief Hydaburg to be a part of the crew that would paddle *Lootaas*, Bill Reid's 50-foot, 1600-pound red cedar canoe, to Haida Gwaii. Cut from a single 700-year-old tree, it had been exhibited at Expo 86 and was the first canoe to be returned to the islands in over a hundred years.

I'd been working with Bill for a while. I remember that he used to get really mad at me because he said I wasn't carving the paddles for his canoe in the right way. I was in my early 20s and I thought I knew it all anyway, but this time I was right. When I practised with the paddles carved the way Bill wanted them, I got blisters all over my hands. I remembered that tsinii Ruben had told me a long time ago, "Just make the paddle as big as your juji and you won't get blisters." So I carved it that way and didn't get one blister on the whole trip paddling from Vancouver to Skidegate!

We did the trip in a week, stopping in villages along the way to be fed and to perform songs and dances in return. We'd always back the canoe onto the beach, as a sign of our peaceful intentions. Chief Hydaburg would then stand in the stern and ask permission of the elders of the village to land. I remember one time we had to stay way offshore because three old ladies in the village didn't want us to land. "You Haida were here before, and you forgot us," they kept saying. They were referring to a time when Haida raiders took members of their families as slaves and left behind three little girls. Those elders were the daughters of those girls. We had to stay out in the water until 4:30 in the morning before they'd let us land.

My brother Archie and my first cousin Woodrow and I were the only three men to do the entire journey. Other crewmembers were changed as we went. I remember Colleen Williams and Nickie Brown were with us for part of the journey. Chief Hydaburg told me that my family was chosen for the whole trip because they should be recognized and honoured for having done many potlatches and were of an important lineage.

After Lionel returned to Vancouver, he continued to sell his argillite sculptures through major art galleries. Robert Giauque, a California art dealer who had seen some of Lionel's work and heard impressive things about the young artist, sought him out. When they met, Bob was immediately struck by the quality of Lionel's work. He began buying

176

188: Lionel's giant *Wasgo* waits, crouched in anticipation, ready to capture his prey: a killer whale. The artist has endowed this supernatural sea wolf with five fins, each tilted in a different direction. Wasgo was so large he could carry dead killer whales in his enormous claws, in the curl of his long tail, and sometimes between his large ears.

189: (facing) Reminiscent of 19th century argillite panel pipes created by past master carvers, Lionel's *Haida Messengers* panel pipe depicts two vaulting killer whales on either side of a pipe bowl. At one end, Frog extends a long tongue to touch the whale's dorsal fin; and at the other end, two ravens exchange tongues. The stem hole of this pipe was drilled from the raven's head on the right. Not actually intended to be smoked, the pipe was created from a single block of argillite. Its intricate forms and remarkable piercings make it an act of carving virtuosity.

his argillite sculptures and in 1997 started advertising them in the prestigious *American Indian Art Magazine.* Lionel had found more than a lucrative pathway to collectors in the U.S. who were interested in contemporary Haida sculpture—he'd found a friend and a patron.

In a personal collection in the States, one of Lionel's orcas vaults above the waves. The fine cross-hatching on the killer whale's body gives the impression of live flesh beneath the stylized formline designs covering the sea mammal's body. The pectoral fins of this supernatural whale are fashioned as raven heads in profile. Lionel's family crest is the three-finned Killer Whale. In the same collection is another sculpture of a five-finned Wasgo or Sea Wolf that, though small in size, is monumental in execution. The carving of this mythical creature's body conveys the tension and power of a hunter ready to spring into action.

Even with great success in selling his art, life in recovery was again filled with ups and downs for Lionel, but he met challenges with humour and no small amount of determination as he continued creating argillite sculptures and building a successful career. In 1999, Lionel met Alice Williamsen, an artist, and they began a life together. Some Haida people affectionately call Alice "Copper Woman." For Lionel, it seemed that his future was evolving as it was intended:

I knew I've always lived the life of a spirited young man and I knew I would get ahead eventually when I grew up and settled down. You have to live life. If you don't have fun it's not worth living. Every day I jump out of bed and say, "Great! I have another day!" I never thought I'd make it out of my teens, then out of my twenties.

Lionel continues to thrive in his personal and artistic life, though he's had a few health-related setbacks. Diagnosed with *ankylosing spon-*

1910: (page 178) *Salmon Feast* moves Lionel's traditional style to the ultra-contemporary with this minimalist design in which parts reveal wholes. The title is the clue to what is being portrayed: a killer whale crashing through a school of salmon, feasting on an abundance of food. By carving only the dorsal fin, the artist layers images for the imagination as he fills one side with two salmon-trout heads symbolizing the salmon that have become a killer whale's dinner.

191: (page 179) On the other side, the killer whale's profile is revealed inside the dorsal fin, his nose turned full circle to press against his tail, toothed mouth open. On the base of the sculpture, three large ovoids with crosshatched inner ovoids represent the salmon eggs that have been released from the salmons' bodies and float, scattered on the water's surface.

dylitis, a particularly painful inflammatory arthritis primarily affecting the spine—a disease that probably claimed the sight of his beloved great grandfather Owt'iwans—Lionel has adapted to a therapeutic regimen that allows him to continue creating sculpture but only if he stands while he carves. He's continually grateful that his sight and his mobility are unaffected.

Though he doesn't consider himself religious, Lionel does have a deep spiritual perspective on his work and his artistic process:

My favourite image when it comes to carving? It's the blank block of argillite sitting in front of me. I've already looked at it and I can see what's inside the stone. I may have to move some parts of the image around, like move a fin, shift a wing or twist a leg in the image, but it's there. If I make a plan, then I can hear God laugh. Every time I try to take the reins, it always ends in a bad way.

Sometimes I'm afraid of the argillite—afraid if I touch it I might wreck it. Then I get into an argument with God; He just says, "Yes. Get on with it. Do it!" That whole part of the process may take an hour or a month, but that's how I start. The first part of carving argillite is two percent creativity; the next part is 98 percent labour. That's the art.

I don't make decisions; I don't draw on the argillite. I just start carving at the top, from the head down and something comes out. The piece is generally finished when it says to me, "Hey! That's enough, that's enough. I'm done." It's not always easy to know if it's done. If I go on too long, the piece gets too busy; if I don't go on long enough, it's too plain. I have to be a carver and a jeweller at the same time.

When I start a piece, I just lose my sense of time. Ten days later, I stop and look and ask, "Wow! Who did that?" It's really not up to me. Sometimes I pretend to know, but I don't really know how any of these things happen.

After learning Lionel's process, looking at his sculptures takes on a deeper meaning. His sculptures range in style from the playful, as seen in the piece he simply calls *Frog*, which reveals a naked woman on its belly, to large elegant argillite replicas of traditional Haida feast dishes, such as the *Raven Stealing the Moon* feast dish lavishly inlaid with cowrie. Lionel is also capable of moving from the literal to surprisingly abstract images, such as his huge *Salmon Feast* that represents an entire visual scenario by only creating the image of a killer whale's fin as the orca crashes through a school of salmon.

Lionel is optimistic about the future of argillite sculpture and his place in it. "Argillite carving is already making an impact among museums and collectors. A lot of people are asking for it, and there are more carvers coming up today," he says, attributing the continuity of interest in argillite sculpture to the work done by Haida artists such as Claude Davidson, the Yeltatzies, and Robert Davidson. He sees part of his role as "making it easier for young carvers to move ahead."

181

192: (upper facing) *Raven Stealing the Light* feast dish. Traditionally, small animal-form bowls were carved in wood and held food or oolichan oil for dipping dried fish. Raven bowls, like this one carved in argillite, are similar to a type of ceremonial regalia known as Raven Rattles. Used by northern Northwest Coast shamans and chiefs, a Raven Rattle resembled a raven in flight. It had a transformation face on its belly, spread wings and a tail with the face of bird-like creature looking towards the raven's head. The transformer, sometimes called Hawk or Thunderbird, had a beak that re-curved into its mouth. Lionel's bowl shares the characteristics of a typical Raven Rattle. Around the rim of the bowl, Lionel has inlaid cowry shells instead of the more traditional opercula that would have been used on the wooden feast dishes.

193, 194: (lower facing) *Transformation Frog* is typical of Lionel's visual surprises. On one side of the sculpture is a frog, and on the reverse the frog's form has been transformed into a woman with human hands and frog feet. Her gender is explicit: she has large drooping breasts and a vagina made from a cowry shell inlaid into the argillite.

195: (above) Lionel always carves standing.

One of Lionel's dreams is to use the land he owns in Old Masset to create a library that would hold documents and argillite collections. "There's nothing like that there now. The village is missing that. I don't need to build a big house; we need a place for honouring argillite artists. I plan to name it *Owt'iwans* after my great grandfather."

Being Haida is as fundamental to Lionel Samuels as the air he breathes, and for that he's grateful:

Howaa. Howaa. It's an honour for me to be a Haida carver and to carry the stories from my nation to the world. I learned that from George Yeltatzie and Claude Davidson when I was growing up. I know they and the people of Haida Gwaii cared enough to keep the culture alive. Now I'm in a position to do my part.

Every morning I thank the Creator for my life as a Haida artist. He's blessed me. Of course, every day I always ask Him for a million dollars! He just laughs and says, "I already gave it to you! It's in your hands. Go carve!"

182

197, 197: *Lionel's Raven Finding Humankind in a Clam Shell* tells a now-familiar story from the time of creation when Raven finds a clam shell filled with the first men on the beach at Naikoon. In this sculptural version of the tale, the humans are clamouring to come out of the shell. At the back of the shell, Lionel has carved a female figure; her vagina is next to the hinge of the clamshell.

198: (pages 184-5) Delbert Smith from the *t'sa. ahl7laanaas* or Double-headed Eagle clan in Old Masset performs as Eagle Dancer.

SCULPTURES AND PORTRAITS

Note: Dimensions are given as **width** x **height** x **depth** facing the main view of the piece.

All dimensions are in centimetres.
Frontispiece: Raven Dancer,
Donnie Edenshaw of the Old Masset
Raven clan
Photo: Jack Litrell

SHAPING STONE

1. Sean Brennan
Journey of the Spirit Canoe (detail:
ovoid)
Argillite with abalone and mastodon
ivory inlay
45 x 16.5 x 13
Private collection
Photo: John W. Heintz

2. Darrell White
Raven and Clam Shell Panel Pipe
(detail)
Argillite with abalone, catlinite, and
18k gold inlay
8.9 x 3.2 x 2.54
Courtesy: Coastal Peoples Fine Arts
Gallery
Photo: John W. Heintz

3. Gary Minaker Russ
*Supernatural Man Who Married the
Eagle King's Daughter* (detail)
Argillite
23 x 30 x 7
Private collection
Photo: Jack Litrell

4. Gary Minaker Russ
Supernatural Strong Man (Su'san)
(detail)
Argillite
15.2 x 15.2 x 8.9
Private collection
Photo: Jack Litrell

5. Donnie Edenshaw
Shark Woman Dancing (detail)
Argillite with abalone
and mastodon ivory inlay
15.2 x 28 x 15.2
Private collection
Photo: John W. Heintz

6. Robert Vogstad
Lazy Son-in-law in the Wasgo Skin
(detail)
Argillite with abalone inlay,
salmon teeth
24 x 20 x4
Courtesy: the artist
Photo: Jack Litrell

7. Marcel Russ
Shaman Torturing a Witch (detail)
Argillite
14 x 27 x 16
Private collection
Photo: Jack Litrell

8. Donnie Edenshaw
Raven Panel Pipe (detail)
Argillite
28 x 8 x 2
Private collection
Photo: Jack Litrell

9. Donnie Edenshaw
Raven Panel Pipe (detail: reverse)
Photo: Jack Litrell

10. Gary Minaker Russ
Thunderbird and Killer Whale (detail:
tail)
Argillite with catlinite and mastodon
ivory inlay
33 x 20.3 x 12.7
base: 15.2 x 30.5 x 7.6
Private Collection
Photo: Jack Litrell

11. Gary Minaker Russ
*Supernatural Man Who Married the
Eagle King's Daughter* (detail: foot)
Photo: Jack Litrell

12. Freddie Wilson
Raven Dancer
Argillite with abalone inlay
15 x 15 x 10
Courtesy: Sarah's Haida Arts and
Jewellery
Photo: Jack Litrell

13. Freddie Wilson
Raven Dancer (reverse)
Photo: Jack Litrell

14. Michael John Brown
Frog Pipe (detail)
Argillite with abalone inlay
28 x 7 x 2.5
Courtesy: Spirits of the West Coast
Native Art Gallery
Photo: Walter Stolting

15. Michael John Brown
Frog Pipe (detail)
Photo: Walter Stolting

16. Darrell White
Legends of the Haida Pole (detail)
Argillite with abalone, catlinite, 18k
gold, and mastodon ivory inlay
7 x 36.2 x 6.9
Courtesy Coastal Peoples Fine Arts
Gallery
Photo: John W. Heintz

17. Darrell White
Haida Legends Pole (detail: reverse)
Photo: John W. Heintz

18. Gary Minaker Russ
Wasgo (detail: signature)
Argillite
14 x 14 x 8
Artist's collection
Photo: John W. Heintz

19. Donnie Edenshaw
Shark Woman Dancing (detail: hands)
Photo: John W. Heintz

BREATH INTO STONE

20–37. Cooper Wilson
Gunarhnesemgyet
Argillite with abalone inlay
39 x 32 x 19 (finished sculpture)
Private collection
Photos by Jack Litrell

COOPER WILSON (b. 1962)

38–39. *Raven Stealing the Light*
Argillite with mastodon ivory and
abalone inlay
75 x 35 x 22
Private collection
Photos: Jack Litrell

40-41. Portraits of Cooper Wilson
Photos: John W. Heintz

42. Cooper Wilson's hands at work
Photo: John W. Heintz

43-44. *Raven Dancer*
Argillite with abalone inlay
17.8 x 19 x 6.4
Courtesy: Masters Gallery Limited
Photos: John W. Heintz

45. Portrait of Cooper Wilson in his
studio
Photo: Jack Litrell

46. *Eagle and Salmon*
Argillite with mastodon ivory and
abalone inlay
16.5 x 22 x 14
Collection: Grace and John Ballem
Photo: John W. Heintz

47. *Raven with Broken Beak*
Argillite with abalone inlay
9.5 x 9.5 x 8.3
Courtesy: Sarah's Haida Arts and
Jewellery
Photo: Walter Stolting

DONNIE EDENSHAW (b. 1978)

48. Donnie Edenshaw as Raven
Dancer. Raven mask and dance
regalia by Donnie Edenshaw
Courtesy: Sarah's Haida Arts and
Jewellery
Photo: Jack Litrell

49. Donnie Edenshaw
with Raven Mask
Raven mask by Donnie Edenshaw
Courtesy: Sarah's Haida Arts and
Jewellery
Photo: Jack Litrell

50. *Raven Panel Pipe*
Argillite
28 x 8 x 2
Private collection
Photo: Jack Litrell

51. *Supernatural Eagle and Salmon*
(detail)
Argillite and bone with abalone inlay
44 x 39 x 23
Private collection
Photo: Jack Litrell

52. *Supernatural Eagle and Salmon*
Photo: John W. Heintz

53. *Supernatural Eagle and Salmon*
(reverse)
Photo: Jack Litrell

54–55. *Shark Woman Dancing*
Argillite
15.2 x 28 x 15.2
Private collection
Photos: Jack Litrell

56. Donnie Edenshaw with daughters
Mya and Sarah
Photo: John W. Heintz

FREDDIE WILSON (b. 1983)

57. *Double-Finned Killer Whale*
Argillite with abalone and mastodon
ivory inlay
24 x 19.5 x 7
Courtesy: Sarah's Haida Arts
and Jewellery
Photo: Jack Litrell

58. Portrait of Freddie Wilson
Photo: John W. Heintz

59. *Bear Bowl*
Argillite with abalone, catlinite,
mastodon ivory, and opercula inlay
29 x 19 x 16.5
Courtesy: the artist
Photo: Jack Litrell

60. *Bear Bowl* and *Skateboard*
Skateboard: Argillite with trade
beads for wheels
7 x 2 (skateboard)
Courtesy: the artist
Photo: John W. Heintz

61-62. *Raven Dancer*
Argillite with abalone inlay
15 x 15 x 10
Courtesy: Sarah's Haida Arts and
Jewellery
Photos: Jack Litrell

63. *Dancing Raven*
Argillite with abalone inlay,
mastodon ivory
19 x 15 x 10
Courtesy: Sarah's Haida Arts and
Jewellery
Photo: Jack Litrell

64. *Panel Pipe*
Argillite with abalone inlay
35 x 7 x 2.3
Courtesy: Sarah's Haida Arts and
Jewellery
Photo: Jack Litrell

SEAN BRENNAN (b. 1982)

65-66. *Bear Father Pole*
8 x 31 x 8
Argillite with abalone inlay
Private collection
Photos: Jack Litrell

67. Portrait of Sean Brennan
Photo: John W. Heintz

68. Richard Widen
*Haida Shaman with Land Otter
Headdress*
Argillite
Dimensions: 6 x 13 x 6
Private collection
Photo: Jack Litrell

69. Sean Brennan carving
Bear Father Pole
Photo: John W. Heintz

70–74. *Journey of the Spirit Canoe*
Argillite with abalone and mastodon
ivory inlay
45 x 16.5 x 13
Private collection
Photos: John W. Heintz

75. *Frog*
6.5 x 2.5 x 5
Argillite with abalone inlay
Courtesy: Sarah's Haida Arts and
Photo: Jack Litrell

MICHAEL JOHN BROWN (b. 1958)

76. Michael John Brown in his
studio
Photo: John W. Heintz

77. Portrait of Michael John Brown
Photo: John W. Heintz

78. Michael John Brown at work on
*Raven Discovering First People in a
Clamshell*
Photo: John W. Heintz

79–80. *Raven Discovering First People
in a Clamshell*
Argillite
17.1 x 12.7 x 10.2
Courtesy: Crystal Cabin Gallery
Photos: Jack Litrell

81. *Frog Pipe*
Argillite with ivory and
mother-of-pearl inlay
28 x 7 x 2.5
Courtesy: Spirits of the West Coast
Native Art Gallery
Photo: Walter Stolting

82. *Haida Stories Panel Pipe*
Argillite with abalone and Mother-of-
Pearl inlay
31.8 x 8.3 x 2.2
Courtesy: Spirits of the West Coast
Native Art Gallery
Photo: Walter Stolting

83. *Chief Bringing Gifts Panel Pipe*
Argillite
29.3 x 8.3 x 2
Courtesy: Crystal Cabin Gallery
Photo: Jack Litrell

84. Michael John Brown's cabin
studio
Photo: John W. Heintz

GRYN WHITE (b. 1977)

85. Portrait of Gryn White and his
family
Photo: John W. Heintz

86–87. *Crest Pole*
Argillite
5.7 x 23.5 x 5
Courtesy: Lattimer Gallery
Photo: John W. Heintz

88. Gryn White's workstation
Photo: John W. Heintz

89–90. *Bear Mother Box*
Argillite with abalone, catlinite, and
mastodon ivory inlay
19 x 21.6 x 15.2
Private collection
Photo: Jeff Gamble

91-93. *Gunarh and the Killer Whale*
Argillite with abalone, catlinite, and
mastodon ivory inlay
26 x 25 x 21 (with base)
Collection: Rick Grange
Photos: Jack Litrell

SHAUN EDGARS (b. 1978)

94. Shaun Edgars at work
Photo: John W. Heintz

95. Portrait of Shaun Edgars
Photo: John W. Heintz

96. Shaun Edgars tool-finishing
Return of the Sockeye
Photo: John W. Heintz

97. *Return of the Sockeye*
Argillite with abalone inlay
36.8 x 15.2 x 6.4
Private collection
Photo: Jack Litrell

98–99. *Sea Grizzly*
Argillite with abalone and mastodon
ivory inlay
10 x 8.25 x 4
Private collection
Photos: John W. Heintz

CHRIS RUSS (b. 1956)

100. Portrait of Chris Russ
Photo: John W. Heintz

101. *Raven Steals the Light*
Argillite with abalone inlay and silver
Diameter: 8.9 cm x 19cm
Courtesy: Masters Gallery Limited
Photo: John W. Heintz

102–103. *Bear Prince Captures the
Woman*
Argillite with abalone and copper
inlay
15.5 x 12.5 x 7
Private collection
Photos: Jack Litrell

104. *Raven Stealing the Sun*
Argillite with abalone inlay
6.4 x 43.2 x 6.4
Private collection
Photo: Jack Litrell

105-106. *Raven with First People*
Argillite
10.2 x 14 x 7.6
Courtesy: Masters Gallery Limited
Photos: John W. Heintz

107. *Eagle Man*
Argillite
7.5 x 15.5 x 7
Courtesy: Crystal Cabin Gallery
Photo: Jack Litrell

108. *Dogfish Woman*
Argillite with abalone inlay
10.2 x 14 x 5.4
Courtesy: Sarah's Haida Arts and
Jewellery
Photo: Jack Litrell

MARTIN WILLIAMS (b. 1960)

109. *Gunarh or Gunarnesemgyet*
Argillite with abalone inlay
13.3 x 15.2 x 5.7
Private collection
Photo: John W. Heintz

110. Portrait of Martin Williams
Photo: John W. Heintz

111–112. *Gunarnesemgyet* (details)
Photos: Jack Litrell

113. Martin Williams scribes argillite
Photo: Jack Litrell

114–115. *Su'san (Strong Man)*
Argillite with abalone inlay
15.2 x 15.2 x 8.9
Courtesy: Masters Gallery Limited
Photos: Jack Litrell

ROBERT VOGSTAD (b. 1963)

116. Robert Vogstad in front of his
painting *We Are What We Eat*
Collection: the artist
Photo: John W. Heintz

117. *Drawing of Three Gogit*
Pencil on sketchbook paper
305 x 229
Collection: the artist
Photo: Jack Litrell

118. *Wolf and Raven*
Argillite
5 x 7 x 4.4
Private collection
Photo: John W. Heintz

119. *Sqa'na or
Supernatural Killer Whale*
Argillite
10.2 x 10.2 x 5.1
Private collection
Photo: John W. Heintz

120–122. *Shaman and Thunderbird*
Argillite with amber and jade inlay
6.4 x 16.5 x 4.4
Private collection
Photos: John W. Heintz

123–126. *Lazy Son-in-law and the
Wasgo Skin*
Argillite with abalone inlay and
salmon teeth
24.1 x 20.3 x 3.8; raspberry
alabaster base: 15.2 x 3.8 x 10.2
Collection: the artist
Photo: Jack Litrell

GARY MINAKER RUSS (b. 1963)

127. Portrait of Gary Minaker Russ
Photo: John W. Heintz

128–130. *Supernatural Strong Man
(Su'san)*
Argillite
29 x 31 x 10; base: 30 x 16 x 35
Private collection
Photo: Jack Litrell

131. Faye Russ
Double-finned Supernatural Shark
Argillite
14.9 x 9.4 x 1.27
Private Collection
Photo: Jack Litrell

132. *Double-Fin Supernatural Shark*
Argillite
13 x 6 x 3.5
Collection: Grace and John Ballem
Photo: John W. Heintz

133-134. *Thunderbird and Killer
Whale*
Argillite with catlinite, salmon teeth,
and mastodon ivory inlay
20.3 x 33 x 12.7; base: 30.5 x 7.6
x 15.2
Private collection
Photos: Jack Litrell

135-137. *Blind Halibut Fisherman*
Argillite; halibut hook pendant:
catlinite, and silver with abalone and
mastodon ivory inlay
Diameter: 13.5cm x 23cm
Private collection
Photos: Jack Litrell

138-140. *Supernatural Man Who
Married the Eagle King's Daughter*
Argillite
23 x 30 x 7; base: 27 x 14 x 32
Private collection
Photos: Jack Litrell

141–142. *Bear Mother Canoe*
Argillite and catlinite
30.5 x 18.4 x 11.4
Courtesy: Douglas Reynolds Gallery
Photos: John W. Heintz

143. Portrait of Gary Minaker Russ
Photo: John W. Heintz

MARCEL RUSS (b. 1973)

144. Portrait of Lori and Marcel
Russ
Photo: John W. Heintz

145–146. *Raven Travelling Box*
Argillite and silver
Diameter: 9.5cm x 12.1cm
Courtesy: Coastal Peoples Fine Arts
Gallery
Photos: John W. Heintz

147. *Dogfish and Shaman Crest Pole*
Argillite
3 x 12.5 x 2.5.
Courtesy: Coastal Peoples Fine Arts
Gallery
Photo: John W. Heintz

148–149. *Shaman Torturing a Witch*
Argillite
14 x 27 x 16
Private collection
Photos: Jack Litrell

150–152. *Creek Woman Pendant*
Argillite, silver, yew wood, catlinite,
abalone
7.75 x 8.75 x 5
Private collection
Photos: Jack Litrell

153–154. *Bear Feast Dish*
Argillite
8.9 x 5.7 x 3.8
Private collection
Photos: John W. Heintz

155. *Five-finned Killer Whale and
Woman Transforming into an Octopus*
Argillite
12.7 x 16.5 x 7.6
Courtesy: Crystal Cabin Gallery
Photo: Jack Litrell

JAY SIMEON (b. 1976)

156–157. Portraits of Jay Simeon
Photos: John W. Heintz

158. Volcano Woman Pendant
Argillite and gold with abalone and
operculum inlay
7.6 x 4.4 x1.25
Private collection
Photo: John W. Heintz

159–160. Beaver's Lake
Argillite with abalone and mastodon
ivory inlay
11.1 x 14.9 x 13.7
Courtesy: Latimer Gallery
Photos: John W. Heintz

161–163. Nanasimgat Box
Argillite and silver
8.6 x 6.4 x8.3
Courtesy: Latimer Gallery (from the
Arthur Steinman collection)
Photos: John W. Heintz

164. Female Shaman Crest Pole
Argillite with abalone and mammoth
ivory inlay
7 x 33 x 8.3
Courtesy: Latimer Gallery
Photo: John W. Heintz

165–166. Bear Feast Bowl
Argillite with abalone and opal inlay
13.3 x 8.3 x 8.9
Courtesy: Latimer Gallery
Photos: John W. Heintz

DARRELL WHITE (b. 1960)

167. Darrell White working on *Raven
and the First Men Rattle Pendant*
Photo: John W. Heintz

168. Portrait of Darrell White
Photo: John W. Heintz

**169–170. Raven and the First Men
Rattle Pendant**
Argillite with abalone, catlinite,
mother-of-pearl, and mastodon ivory
inlay; 18k gold wire
5.7 x 3.2 x 1.9
Private collection
Photos: John W. Heintz

171. Between Worlds (Soulcatcher)
Argillite with abalone, catlinite, and
mastodon ivory inlay
25.4 x 7.6 x 6.4
Private collection
Photo: John W. Heintz

172. Killer Whale Clan Pendant
Argillite with abalone, catlinite, 18k
gold, and mammoth ivory inlay
2.5 x 6.4 x 2.5
Courtesy: Coastal Peoples Fine Arts
Gallery
Photo: John W. Heintz

173–175. Kerfed Chief's Box
Argillite with abalone, catlinite and
18k gold inlay
16.5 x 12.7 x 12.1
Private collection
Photos: John W. Heintz

176. Raven and Clam Shell Panel Pipe
Argillite with abalone, catlinite, and
18k gold inlay
8.9 x 3.2 x 2.54
Courtesy: Coastal Peoples Fine Arts
Gallery
Photo: John W. Heintz

177–179. Darrell White at work and
his workspace
Photos: John W. Heintz

**180–182. Legends of the
Haida Crest Pole**
Argillite with abalone, catlinite, 18k
gold, and mastodon ivory inlay
7 x 36.2 x 6.9
Courtesy: Coastal Peoples
Fine Arts Gallery
Photos: John W. Heintz

LIONEL SAMUELS (b. 1963)

183. Portrait of Alice Williamsen
and Lionel Samuels
Photo: John W. Heintz

**184. Supernatural Raven-finned Killer
Whale**
Argillite with abalone inlay
11.4 x 27.9 x 5.7
Private collection
Photo: Robert Giauque

185. Lionel Samuels Carving
Photo: John W. Heintz

**186-187. Raven Stealing the Light
Dancer**
Argillite with abalone inlay
15.2 x 27.9 x 10.2
Collection: Gary Piaget
Photos: Gary Piaget

188. Sea Wolf or **Wasgo**
Argillite
20.3 x 20.3 x 8.9
Private collection
Photo: Robert Giauque

189. Haida Messengers Panel Pipe
Argillite with abalone inlay
52.1 x 7.6 x 2.54
Courtesy: Coastal Peoples Fine Arts
Gallery
Photo: John W. Heintz

190–191. Salmon Feast
Argillite with abalone inlay
26.7 x 28.6 x 7
Collection: Gary Piaget
Photos: John W. Heintz

**192. Raven Stealing the
Light Feast Dish**
Argillite with cowry shell inlay
33 x 14.6 x 13.3
Private collection
Photo: Robert Giauque

193–194. Transformation Frog
Argillite with abalone, catlinite and
cowry inlay
15.2 x 6.4 x 17.8
Private collection
Photos: Robert Giauque

195. Portrait of Lionel Samuels
Photo: John W. Heintz

**196–197. Raven Finding
Humankind in a Clam Shell**
Argillite with abalone inlay
14 x 22.9 x 12.7
Private collection
Photos: John W. Heintz

**Front cover: Shaman Torturing a
Witch** by Marcel Russ
Photo: Jack Litrell

Back cover: Sean Brennan carving
Bear Father Pole
Photo: John W. Heintz
Author photo: Sophia K. Browne

Frontispiece pages 2-3: Raven
Dancer Donnie Edenshaw on the
beach at Naikoon with daughters
Mya and Sarah
Photo: Jack Litrell

**Closing photo spread pages
184-185:** Eagle Dancer Delbert
Smith of the *T'sa.ahl7laanaas* or
Double-headed Eagle clan
Photo: Jack Litrell

BIBLIOGRAPHY

Augaitis, Daina, et al. 2006. *Raven Travelling: Two Centuries of Haida Art.* Vancouver: Vancouver Art Gallery.

Barbeau. Marius. 1950. *Totem Poles.* Bulletin 119. Vols. 1 and 2, Anthropological Series No. 30. Ottawa: National Museums of Canada.

— 1953. *Haida Myths Illustrated in Argillite Carvings.* Bulletin 127, Anthropological Series No. 32. Ottawa: Department of Resources and Development, National Parks Branch, National Museums of Canada.

— 1957. *Haida Carvers in Argillite.* Bulletin 139, Anthropological Series No. 38. Ottawa: Department of Resources and Development, National Parks Branch, National Museums of Canada.

Blackman, Margaret B. 1982. *During My Time: Florence Edenshaw Davidson, a Haida Woman.* Seattle: University of Washington Press.

Dockstader, Frederick. 1962. "Kwawhlhal Carvings from Skidegate" in *Natural History,* 71: 30-39.

Drew, Leslie and Douglas Wilson. 1980. *Argillite Art of the Haida.* North Vancouver: Hancock House Publishers Ltd.

Duff, Wilson, and Michael Kew. 1958. "Anthony Island, A Home of the Haidas" in *British Columbia Provincial Museum Annual Report for 1957.* 37-64.

Duff, Wilson 1964. The Indian History of British Columbia. *Anthropology in British Columbia.* Vol. 1. Memoir No. 5.

— 1967. "Contexts of Northwest Coast Art" in *Arts of the Raven.* Vancouver: Vancouver Art Gallery.

Duff, Wilson, Bill Holm and Bill Reid. 1967. *Arts of the Raven.* Vancouver: Vancouver Art Gallery.

Enrico, John. 2003. *Haida Dictionary.* Juneau: Sealaska Heritage Institute and Alaska Native Center.

Harrison, Charles. 1911-1913. History of the Queen Charlotte Islands: The Haida and their Legends. *Queen Charlotte Islander.* Vol. 1, No. 11 through Vol. 2, No.14.

— 1925. *Ancient Warriors of the North Pacific: The Haida, Their Laws, Customs and Legends, with Some Historical Account of the Queen Charlotte Islands.* London: H.F. and G. Witherby.

Holm, Bill. 1965. *Northwest Coast Indian Art: An Analysis of Form.* Seattle: University of Washington Press.

MacDonald, George F. 1983. *Haida Monumental Art: Villages of the Queen Charlotte Islands.* Vancouver: University of British Columbia.

Macnair, Peter and Alan Hoover. 1984. *The Magic Leaves: A History of Haida Argillite Carving.* Victoria: British Columbia Provincial Museum.

Macnair, Peter, Alan Hoover and Kevin Neary. 1980. *The Legacy: Continuing Traditions of Canadian Northwest Coast Indian Art.* Victoria: British Columbia Provincial Museum.

Niblack, A.P. 1888. *The Coast Indians of Southern Alaska and Northern British Columbia.* Washington, D.C.

Sheehan, Carol. 1981. *Pipes that Won't Smoke; Coal That Won't Burn.* Calgary: Glenbow Museum.

Stewart, Hilary. 1993. *Looking at Totem Poles.* Seattle: University of Washington Press.

Swanton, John R. 1905a. *Contributions to the Ethnology of the Haida.* Leiden and New York: E.J. Brill and G.E. Stechert.

— 1905b. *Haida Texts and Myths, Skidegate Dialect.* New York: Bureau of American Ethnology.

— 1908. *Haida Texts: Masset Dialect.* Leiden: E.J. Brill.

Swanton, John R., and Franz Boas (eds.). 1912. *Haida Songs and Tsimshian Texts.* Publications of the American Ethnological Society, Vol. 3. Leiden: E.J. Brill.

Wardwell, Allen. 1978. *Objects of Bright Pride: Northwest Coast Indian Art from the American Museum of Natural History.* New York: The Center for Inter-American Relations and the American Federation of Arts.

Wright, Robin K. 2001. *Northern Haida Master Carvers.* Seattle: University of Washington Press.

INDEX